MEANINGFUL AGING

HOW MINDSET MAKES IT HAPPEN

Harnessing the power of our dynamic mindset to achieve fulfillment in our golden years

BALDEV K. SEEKRI

Visit our website at www.StillwaterPress.com for more information.

First Stillwater River Publications Edition

Library of Congress Control Number: 2020906314

ISBN-13: 978-1-952-52106-5

1 2 3 4 5 6 7 8 9

Written by Baldev Seekri
Published by Stillwater River Publications, Pawtucket, RI, USA.

Publisher's Cataloging-In-Publication Data
(Prepared by The Donohue Group, Inc.)

Names: Seekri, Baldev K., author.
Title: Meaningful aging : how mindset makes it happen ; harnessing the power of our dynamic mindset to achieve fulfillment in our golden years / Baldev K. Seekri.
Description: First Stillwater River Publications edition. | Pawtucket, RI, USA : Stillwater River Publications, [2020]
Identifiers: ISBN 9781952521065 | ISBN 1952521068
Subjects: LCSH: Self-actualization (Psychology) in old age. | Older people--Psychology. | Aging--Psychological aspects. | Older people--Life skills guides.
Classification: LCC BF724.85.S45 S445 2020 | DDC 155.67--dc23

The views and opinions expressed in this book are solely those of the author and do not necessarily reflect the views and opinions of the publisher.

Dedicated to

All seniors who are striving to find meaning
in the last phase of their human existence.

Contents

Acknowledgements

As I conclude the writing of Meaningful Aging, I am overwhelmed with feelings of admiration and gratitude for 10 remarkable seniors, without whom this book would have never materialized. Spanning the globe and embodying diverse walks of life, Dr. Paul J Maryan, Air Marshal Raghavendran, Dolores Cummins, Viswakant Mankodi, Mai Donohue, Carol Young, Dr. Dinesh O. Shah, Enrique Brouwer, Vijaya Srinivasan and Dr. Thomas Mathew have enriched this book by sharing their personal mindsets about aging meaningfully and joyfully. These extraordinary people have become my role models and cherished friends for life.

In addition to these remarkable seniors, my heartfelt thanks go out to many great authors for precious insights from their books, which have been instrumental in keeping Meaningful Aging an objective and stimulating presentation. Special thanks to Jo Ann Jenkins, CEO of AARP and author of Disrupt Aging: Living Your Best Life at Every Age; the late Dr. Gene Cohen, author of the Creative Age: Awakening Human Potential in the Second Half of Life; Carol Dweck, author of Mindset: the New Psychology of Success; Atul Gawande, author of Being Mortal: Medicine and What Matters in the End; and my mentor, the late Dr. Judith Bardwick, author of Danger in The Comfort Zone: From Boardroom to Mailroom — How to Break the Entitlement Habit That's Killing American Business and many others.

I also owe a debt of gratitude to many brave seniors who participated in discussions about the contents of this book and shared their very personal challenges and hopes. Their exchanges, like the ones mentioned in the epilogue, provided real-life experiences that will serve as beneficial examples for many other seniors.

I feel very fortunate to have met Laura Meade Kirk, a former reporter and bureau manager for the Providence Journal, who taught me how to convey the messages in this book crisply and clearly. She was a hard teacher, but nevertheless a great editor.

I am exceedingly grateful to Srinivas Thalluru, quality assurance engineer at Retail Solutions Inc., for his dedicated support in configuring the graphics and images presented in this book, as well as facilitating the completion of this book on time.

There aren't enough words to thank my loving wife, Kamlesh, for her unflinching support and encouragement to me while writing this book. She was my biggest supporter as well as my most objective critic, and she kept me balanced in my thinking and articulation.

Finally, breaking all standards of conventional wisdom and political correctness, I earnestly wish to thank myself for keeping my dynamic mindset of aging loyal to my purposeful passion of ceaseless learning and sharing my knowledge with others. Continuing to meet my commitment of writing a new book every five years, I am watching my legacy grow, which in turn makes my personal life journey meaningful and joyful.

Introduction

The Golden Age had finally arrived!

Newly retired from Texas Instruments in 2005, I often fantasized about the glory of my hard-earned golden years, looking forward to a life of sheer tranquility. My time would be my own, no longer dictated by a schedule crammed with corporate meetings and tight deadlines to be met. Such was the reward I had earned after 30 years as a successful executive with a global technology company, and I was anxiously looking forward to enjoying my newly found freedom. Little did I know that a simple question posed to me by a stranger in a casino would transform my vision of golden tranquility into a nightmare.

A few months after bidding farewell to the corporate world, a friend had asked me to join him for an outing at a nearby casino. While exchanging pleasantries with a neatly dressed middle-aged stranger sitting next to me at the blackjack table, this gentleman casually asked, "What do you do?"

"I am retired," I responded, speaking loudly so I could be heard over the clattering of coins and clanging bells from the nearby slot machines.

"That is really great," the stranger replied, adding enviously, "I wish I could retire, but it is going to take a long time for me to get there."

After a brief silence, he asked again, "So, what *did* you do?" I explained that I had retired about six months before after 30 years of managing different business divisions within my company. I was now enjoying the freedom of retirement; of having no set schedule and being able to do whatever I wanted — including coming here to the casino for a game of cards.

"Lucky you," the stranger said, with a deep sigh. "What a great company you worked for and what a great career you had. Few people can say that these days."

I had hoped that was the end of the conversation, but instead he persisted: *"So, what do you do?"*

Having already answered him previously, I didn't bother to respond. But for some reason, the question nagged at me from that point on. Unable to concentrate on my cards, I was losing money. Frustrated and somewhat annoyed by the stranger's repetitive questioning, I politely excused myself to find another table at which to play.

In the ensuing weeks, I found myself dwelling on that encounter, though I wasn't entirely sure why. Was it the incivility of the stranger and his irksome questions? Or was it my inability to think of a suitable riposte? My uneasiness increased as the weeks went on, especially when I started to hear the same question from others, including well-known acquaintances: *"What do you do?"*

There seemed to be no fitting response. I could explain what I used to do during my successful career at Texas Instruments and the many marvelous experiences I had there. Or I could talk about enjoying the freedom of retirement, including spending time with my wife and my grown children, especially my granddaughters, and visiting with other relatives as well. However, neither response seemed particularly appropriate to that simple yet tormenting question: *"What do you do?"*

Then one day I realized that, absorbed by the tranquility of my retired life, I had lost the very essence of me — that definable sense of identity, of purpose, that set me apart from others — especially while I was so focused on enjoying my carefree lifestyle.

For the next two years, I embarked on a mission to create a new identity for myself. I was ready to do anything, as peculiar as it may be. I invested a good part of my savings to purchase a fast-food Indian restaurant, but it closed less than 18 months later, at a significant financial loss. I took risks on some other business ventures, with even less financial success.

So here I was, two years after being confounded by that nagging question from a stranger, with my savings partially annihilated, and I was no closer to finding my new identity. I started to doubt my own sanity as I confronted the reality of aging in retirement.

Dejected, I sought refuge in thoughts of my pre-retirement days, indulging in a serious reflection of the triumphs and tribulations of my professional career and life. Lo and behold, after reflecting for a few weeks, I discovered a truth that was at once both jarring and inspiring.

The Truth: Many, if not most, people approach retirement far differently than any other phases of their lives. They develop an enigmatic mindset about aging, focused on existing rather than living with meaning and purpose. This flawed mindset causes them to spend their well-deserved golden years chasing freedom and entitlement, only to find themselves feeling helpless when they realize they were chasing something they couldn't attain.

Reflecting on my past helped me realize that I had overlooked the mindset of living with meaning and purpose that had helped fuel my success and happiness while I was working; the sense of fulfillment that comes with accomplishing something worthwhile, while continuing to grow as a person and contributing to the welfare of others and society at large. It was the power of this mindset that had empowered me to achieve the many milestones of my life with tremendous success and an enviable sense of identity, both at work and in my personal life. Somehow, the deceptive glare of the golden years had caused me to lose sight of this most important perspective, a longtime ally, without which my retirement and aging seemed aimless and meaningless.

Rejuvenated by the realization of what was lacking in my retired life, I started to ponder my passions, trying to identify those that would enable me to live my golden years with meaning and purpose. It didn't take long for me to discover that my passions for learning and sharing my knowledge could serve as that enabler to generate fulfillment. So, in 2008, nearly three years into my retirement, I decided to write a book based on my professional experience of successfully transforming poorly performing businesses into benchmark enterprises. That book, *Organizational Turnarounds with a Human Touch,* was published in late 2011, and it established a new identity for me: **a published author.**

My first book not only rekindled and enhanced my passion for learning and sharing knowledge, but it also became instrumental in positively affecting many people and organizations. One of those people was Mike Ritz, the executive director of Leadership Rhode Island, a nationally recognized community leadership development organization. After reading my book, Mike was so impressed with what he had learned from my experiences, that he asked me to join the board of governors of his organization. I served on the board for six years, during which time I helped direct many of the initiatives that led to the organization's growth and profitability.

Energized by having discovered this path to making my retirement years more meaningful and joyful, I embarked on writing a second book, which was published in 2017. *Seizing Success: How Mindset Makes It Happen* offers a fresh look at the meaning of success based on my personal experiences and the stories of seven other people of various ages and backgrounds who also achieved success in each of their chosen pursuits. That book was so well-received that I was encouraged to write this, my third book, *Meaningful Aging: How Mindset Makes It Happen,* to help others struggling to find purpose and passion in their retirement years.

Our definition of retirement has changed significantly in the last 100 years. When the Social Security Act passed in 1935, the official retirement age was 65. Back then, the average life expectancy was 58. Thanks largely to advances in modern medicine, life expectancy has increased dramatically since then. Even those who postpone retirement for personal or financial reasons often live for years after leaving the workforce, with many of today's retirees living well into their 80s and 90s – and beyond.

During the 15 years since my retirement, I have observed that the initial thrill of retirement doesn't last long for most retirees. After the first few years of freedom, the three plagues of old age – boredom, isolation and helplessness – often start to set in. Lacking focus or purpose, the idea of a protracted life after retirement can seem unbearable, burdensome and joyless. To avoid this unfortunate outcome, seniors need to adopt a new mindset of aging and commit to living their golden years with meaning and purpose.

There are countless books on aging, but most seem to focus on managing the financial aspects of retirement or the methodology of living a long and healthy life. However, they fail to address a more fundamental piece of the puzzle: our mindset toward aging and, more specifically, our attitudes about growing older.

While the financial and health aspects of aging are undoubtedly essential elements, it is our mindset that ultimately will determine the quality of our lives as we age and will serve as the foundation for our emotional happiness and well-being. A flawed mindset based upon ignorance and unrealistic expectations of our golden years could lead to a long, meaningless journey, ending in disappointment. However, developing and deploying a proper mindset towards aging can lead to a thrilling adventure and abundant gratification in the last years of our lives.

There is more to aging than managing the physical and financial aspects; the right mindset is critical to achieving emotional happiness and well-being.

This book will provide a path to meaningful and joyful aging in retirement by helping you develop the right mindset. We will start by answering the following questions:

- What is aging, anyway?
- How can we make the last phase of our lives the most fulfilling?
- What type of mindset will help us to achieve our goals?

In the first section of the book, we will seek answers to these vital questions and develop a meaningful archetype for aging that is capable of guiding us to fulfillment in the last phase of our life. We will examine the experiences of five remarkable seniors who are living proof of the validity of each element of this archetypal mindset.

In the second section of the book, we will see our meaningful mindset in action. We will hear from five seniors who share their personal life stories, explaining how they discovered new paths to personal fulfillment after retiring by developing the right mindset and using most, if not all, elements of our archetypal mindset. Their stories serve as validation for our model and provide information and ideas that will prove useful in helping us develop and maintain a healthy mindset towards our own meaningful aging.

These ten seniors from first and the second sections, who have achieved success and fulfillment in their personal, professional and retired lives, represent diverse cultural values and beliefs spanning the Americas,

Europe, Asia and Australia. The six men and four women range in age from the early 60s to the early 90s. Prior to retiring, their professional backgrounds ran the gamut: private industry, education, journalism, military and medicine.

In the third section of the book, we will explore how to implement strategies learned in the first two sections by following what I call the *Five Mandates for Developing Your Mindset for Meaningful Aging,* a step-by-step guide that will help you develop a dynamic mindset and chart your own path to personal fulfillment in your final years. While it may be tempting to skip that section first, you will be missing much of the valuable information provided in the first two sections, including the priceless wisdom offered by our five role models.

The goal of this book is simple: to convince you that the proper mindset is vitally important to the aging process. We all have the choice whether to merely exist or to live with meaning and purpose, which will give us satisfaction and fulfillment in our final years.

Section 1

A Dynamic Mindset
of Meaningful Aging

Chapter 1

What Is Aging, Anyway?

Age is an issue of mind over matter.

If you don't mind, it doesn't matter.

— Mark Twain

"Is there a way for us to simply fold our hands, say goodbye and be gone?"

That question, posed to me by a friend in his late 70s, sent a shudder down my spine and led me to question my personal perspective toward the final chapter of my life.

It was the fall of 2015 and I was 75 years old. Having retired a decade before, after what my friends and colleagues described as an enormously successful corporate career, I was basking in the glory of my golden years. I had published a book and was serving on the board of governors for a statewide community leadership development organization when this fateful meeting with my friend transpired.

Several years older than me, I had known him for most of my adult life. He was the embodiment of success in his professional and personal life, and I considered him a role model, frequently seeking his advice for many challenges I had faced in my life. Ironic, then, that while chatting with him during a get-together with friends, I would hear those words of despair from someone who had achieved incredible success throughout the many milestones of his long life.

Anxious to discern his predicament, I gently prodded to learn the meaning behind such a dramatic statement. "Jay, I never thought I would

1

hear these words from anyone, but especially not from you. Are you joking?"

"Not a bit," he replied.

"Are you all right, physically and emotionally?" I asked, somewhat apprehensively.

"No worse than anyone else my age," he said.

His apathy further amplified my worry. I reminded him of the enduring openness of our friendship and beseeched him to share any issues or concerns he might have.

"Baldev, I am through. There is nothing left to accomplish and every day is a futile passage of time," he responded, flatly.

"Jay, you still have a long life ahead of you, with plenty of time to make yet another mark," I said. I hoped my words could somehow rekindle the spark of curiosity and ingenuity that had led to so many of his previous successes.

Instead, he shrugged me off. "I am just waiting for this to be over," he said. "There is no fun living in isolation; in being seen as useless and helpless. I have started to see myself as a liability to my friends and family, and I foresee my remaining days as nothing more than a burden for them and slow torture for me."

After uttering those disheartening words, he walked away, melding into the crowd of other guests, leaving me dumbfounded and sad.

As I pondered that depressing encounter with my friend, I thought of other retirees I had encountered over the past 10 years. I realized that my friend's situation was not that unusual; it mirrored the experience of so many other seniors over age 65 who often find themselves feeling caught in what they believe to be a whirlpool of societal disdain and self-pity.

Many of them view aging in a negative light, often describing themselves and others with terms such as:

- Limited
- Burdensome
- Jaded
- Helpless
- Desolate

Some of you reading this book may feel this way yourself – and you are not alone. After a few years of retirement, many seniors adopt these negative stereotypes of themselves.

How ironic that this last chapter of our lives – arguably one of the most important periods of human life – is often viewed as cursed rather than cherished.

However, these perceptions of old age as a nightmare and of seniors being an unwanted burden on society contribute to the negative stereotypes of seniors often been viewed as outcasts rather than essential, contributing members of society.

When and How Did the Elderly Become Pariahs?

Not long ago, in the early 1900s, seniors were revered as vital members of their communities, generally cared for until their last breath by multi-generational members of their own families, especially back in the day when families tended to live close together, in the same homes or at least nearby, as generations before them had done.

Of course, people did not live as long back then. According to data from the National Institute on Aging, the average life expectancy in the United States in 1900 was 47 years. At the beginning of the 20th century, in the absence of antibiotics and preventative medicine, people often died quickly from as a result of accident, illness or disease.

However, after World War II, sweeping advances in medicine and technology, coupled with an increase in social welfare programs such as Social Security and Medicare, contributed to a radical increase in life expectancy through the end of the century. At the same time, societal changes that resulted in more families living apart led to an increase in residential and medical facilities to accommodate the increasing number of seniors living independently or relying on non-family members to care for them as they aged. All the while, the average life expectancy continued to increase, with the average American living to age 77 by the year 2016.

Increasing Life Expectancy in USA

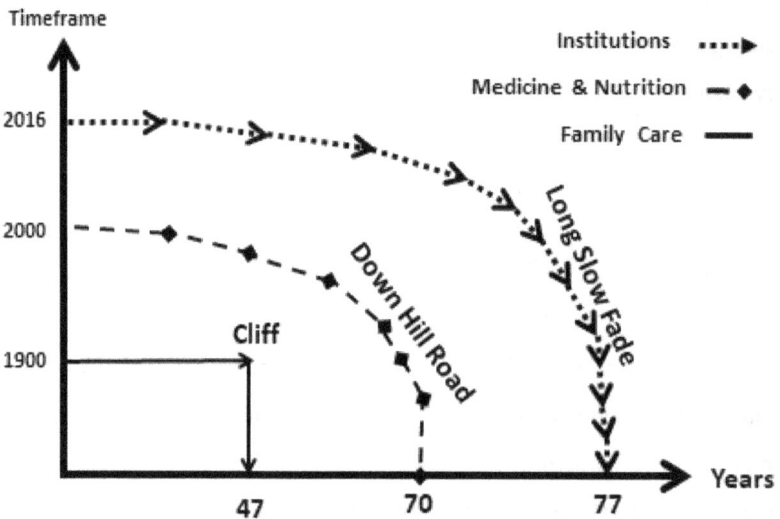

Timeframe

Institutions ....▶
Medicine & Nutrition ━◆
Family Care ━━

2016

2000

Cliff

1900

Down Hill Road

Long Slow Fade

Years

47   70   77

This increase in life expectancy has impacted society in other ways, as well. Consider this: by the year 2015, there were as many men and women over age 80 as there were children under age 5. Compare this to 1950, when there was only one senior over age 80 for every 11 children under age 5.

As life expectancy continues to increase, living to age 80 or more is no longer unusual; in fact, the number of people who live to age 90 or more has grown dramatically in recent years. The National Institutes of Health reported that the number of people over age 90 more than doubled at the turn of the century – from 720,000 in 1980 to 1.9 million 2010. This number is projected to grow to 9 million seniors over age 90 by the year 2050.

This explosion in the population of seniors in America and other developed countries appears to have taken everyone off guard – from those living longer to society as a whole. Although most people cherish the notion of living a longer life, few seem prepared to deal with it effectively. As time marches on, our society is struggling to meet the increased demands posed by the aging population. At the same time, many seniors are not properly prepared or equipped to live longer than they originally anticipated, often leaving them feeling lost and alone, especially if they have no family members to care for them. So, it is understandable that many seniors, like my friend Jay, feel that they simply want to fold their hands, say a final goodbye and be gone.

The increasing growth in the population of seniors, coupled with the demands this places on their family members and society as a whole, has contributed to an overall change in attitude towards seniors, who often are no longer viewed as indispensable assets but rather potential liabilities. The reverence once bestowed on those who had reached a certain age has evolved into a sense of indifference or, worse, intolerance in many cases.

Unwitting Co-conspirators

Are seniors victims of societal backlash because of the explosion in the aging population and the burdens this generation now represents? On the surface, they may seem to be innocent victims of this cultural evolution. However, a deeper dive into the root cause of this issue shows that they may be unwitting co-conspirators in generating some of these unfortunate negative stereotypes.

To understand this, consider the analogy of a team competing in a sporting event with four quarters of play. If the players approach the game with the mindset that they will learn, adapt and excel in the first three quarters and relax in the final quarter, believing their momentum alone will lead them to victory, they may be surprised to find themselves losing the game in the end. They likely would become sore losers and blame their loss on bad luck or unfair tactics by the other team. On the contrary, if the players go into the game with the mindset of learning, adapting and excelling in all four quarters — especially during the fourth and final quarter, when they are physically and emotionally exhausted — they are likely to greatly increase their chance of winning. Some of the greatest championships in sports history are won in the final quarter of the match; in fact, many come down to the last few minutes of the game.

Too many seniors approach retirement and old age like the players on the team that had no solid plan for the final quarter of their game, other than to relax and enjoy themselves and count on their previous momentum to carry them to the end. They believe they deserve a carefree life as a reward for a lifetime of hard work and the sacrifices they have made over the years. Assuming they have the financial resources to carry them through, they look forward to their remaining time as their leisure years or golden years. They see retirement as the holy grail, their vision of heaven on earth, and they focus solely on their belief that they have earned every right to be there.

It doesn't take long for them to realize that most of their dreams of retirement do not reflect reality; in fact, many people discover a void in their lives as their golden years start to tarnish. They may relish their freedom and leisure time for a few years, but they also may find themselves struggling with issues they may not have anticipated. It may be the lost sense of identity or self-worth now that they no longer have a career. Or perhaps they are not used to spending so much time with a spouse or partner, leading to irritation. They may face financial burdens while living on a fixed income or because of bad decisions or failed ventures borne of an endeavor to kill time. Health and mobility issues also impact retirement dreams and goals. Many retirees find themselves feeling nostalgic, longing for the way things used to be. All of these factors can generate confusion and stress, adversely impacting a person's attitudes and behaviors. Combined, these contribute to the specific negative stereotypes mentioned in the beginning of this chapter.

With few exceptions, most retirees fall into this trap because of their ignorance about the following realities (truths) about aging:

- Aging is a lifelong process – not just for the elderly
- Aging is about living – not ceasing to live
- We cannot stop aging, but we can choose how to age
- We continue to create and/or cement our legacies until aging ends

Aging is Not for the Elderly Only

Most people don't grow up. Most people age.
— Maya Angelou

Aging is not a curse for the elderly; it is a natural gift for all – whether a child, an adult and or a senior. Judith Horstman, an award-winning journalist explains this in her book, *The Scientific American Healthy Aging*

7

Brain: The Neuroscience of Making the Most of Your Mature Mind.

In her book, Ms. Horstman writes: *Aging is much broader than the white-haired, wrinkled, cane-toting physical and mental debility most people associate with "getting old." The process actually takes place on multiple levels, every second of every day.* She goes on to describe three phases of aging that include outward physical changes, such as wrinkles and stooped posture; internal changes within our organs, including atrophy or degeneration of the brain; and microscopic changes that occur within the cells of our bodies. These changes take place in everyone, at every age, from childhood through old age.

Beyond the physical changes, aging also involves a series of psychological and emotional changes that occur in every age. We see this in our own families, including mine. I recall a recent encounter with my granddaughter, Asha, who at the time was 18 months old. My wife, Kamlesh, and I had returned to the Northeast after spending the winter in Florida. We hadn't seen Asha in several months, so she was understandably apprehensive when my wife approached with outstretched arms, seeking to give her a hug. Instead, Asha ran off and hid behind her mother – just as her mother, our daughter, Tina, used to do when she was that age.

What does this simple example of the interaction between my wife and granddaughter have to do with the complex subject of aging? A lot! Everyone, including our daughter and granddaughter, goes through a series of developmental and psychological changes as they age and mature. This process is best explained by the late Erik Erikson, a renowned psychoanalyst who is credited with reshaping views of human development.

In his widely acclaimed theory of psychosocial development, Mr. Erikson explains eight key phases that occur throughout the life cycle, from birth through death. Each phase presents challenges and crises that must be successfully resolved and/or achieved to prepare us for success in the next phase of our social development.

While he cites eight phases of development, for the purposes of this book, I have selected five that I believe critical to consider in our discussion of the aging process. The chart below outlines the challenges posed during each of these phases and the virtues learned.

Age	Psychosocial Crises	Virtues
Infancy 0-18 months	Trust vs. Mistrust	Hope
Early Childhood 2-4 years	Autonomy vs. Shame/Doubts	Will
Early Adulthood 20-39 years	Intimacy vs. Isolation	Love
Adulthood 40-64 years	Stagnation	Care
Maturity 65-death	Ego/Integrity vs. Despair	Wisdom

During infancy, a child who develops a trusted relationship with a parent or caregiver develops a sense of hope that ideally leads to success in subsequent phases of social development. Similarly, in early adulthood, an individual learns to develop healthy relationships leading to committed, lasting relationships with those they love.

The final phase involves the late stages of adulthood, when people reflect on their lives. Those who look back with a sense of satisfaction will be blessed with a sense of wisdom, fulfillment and integrity. Those who have regrets are more likely to have a bleak outlook, marked with bitterness and despair.

As we have learned through the works of Judith Horstman, Erik Erikson and others, it is clear that aging is not for the elderly alone, but rather part of our physical and emotional development at every phase of human life. Aging is a process that begins at childbirth and continues until our final breath. Understanding this truth is vital for everyone, at every age.

Aging is a lifetime of physical change and emotional development — not a path to doom for the elderly.

Aging is living not ceasing to live

> With mirth and laughter let old wrinkles come.
> — William Shakespeare

A few years ago, while chatting with some of the residents who live in the retirement community in Florida where my wife and I spend our winters, I was struck by the vastly different tones of our discussions. One gentleman was 86 and happily retired. He was making plans to start a discussion group to find ways to improve the quality of life for himself and others living there. Another was 72 and clearly not enjoying himself at all. He said each day was a struggle for him, adding: "Every morning, I pray: *Please God, take me away.*"

Fast-forward to this year, four years after that initial conversation, and the first gentleman is still in high spirits, looking much younger than his 90 years. He not only launched that discussion group, but also followed up by initiating a string of other activities that include book discussion groups, presentations by speakers on various topics, community safety initiatives and more.

The second person is now 76 and still praying every day for God to take him away. His prayer hasn't yet been answered, but there's little doubt that his bitterness and whining have contributed greatly to the decline in his physical appearance, causing him to look much older than he actually is.

Many seniors seem to view their final years as he does — as a slow, cruel fade into the inevitable end of their lives. But others embrace the positive attitude espoused by Jo Ann Jenkins, Chief Executive Officer of AARP, in her book, *Disrupt Aging: A Bold New Path to Living Your Best Life at Every Age*, in which she writes: *We don't stop and withdraw from society because we become a certain age. We understand that some aspects of life get a little tougher and some get a little easier as we get older, but it's all part of living, and we are determined to make the most of it. In short, we reflect the new reality of aging — it's all about living.*

Throughout history, many seniors who embraced the notion of continuing to live and grow as they aged went on to achieve amazing feats:

- **Anna Mary Robertson Moses**, a self-taught artist best known as **Grandma Moses**, first started painting in her late 70s because arthritis prevented her from pursuing her favorite pastime of embroidering. By the time she died in 1961 at age 101, her paintings had been displayed in fine art galleries throughout the United States and Europe.

- Internationally renowned Spanish cellist, conductor and composer **Pablo Casals** was 95 years old when he conducted an impassioned musical tribute to peace before the United Nations in 1971, when he was presented with the organization's Peace Medal.

- At age 84, **Dr. Benjamin Spock**, a world-renowned pediatrician and advocate for social justice, was among dozens of people arrested while participating in a 1988 protest march on Capitol Hill to raise awareness for the plight of the homeless.

- At age 81, **Benjamin Franklin** was the oldest delegate to the 1787 Constitutional Convention, where he helped broker the compromise that led to the adoption of the U.S. Constitution.

- German gymnast **Johanna Quass** was 86 years old when the Guinness Book of World Records certified her as the oldest gymnast in the world in 2012. As of last fall, she still held that title at age 93.

- **Fred Mack**, a retired engineer from New Jersey, is believed to have set a world record as the oldest skydiver after celebrating his 100th birthday by jumping from a plane. (It was the second time he'd ever skydived; the first time was on his 95th birthday.)

- At age 90, **Eamon de Valera** was still serving as president of Ireland.

- **Michelangelo** was overseeing the design and construction of St. Peter's Basilica in Rome until his death at age 88 in 1564. Fourteen years before, the Catholic Church begged him to come out of retirement to help finish the project, which had languished for years. It wasn't completed until after his death.

- At age 96, **Mohr Keet** of South Africa set the Guinness World Record for being the oldest person to bungee jump. That was in 2010.

- **Dr. Leila Denmark**, a Georgia pediatrician, was the oldest practicing physician in the country when she retired in 2005 at the age of 103.

Retirement offers an extended opportunity for living and accomplishing something worthwhile.

For those of us who are retired or approaching retirement, it is imperative that we understand and embrace this truth – that we can continue to live and achieve. Oprah Winfrey, the legendary television actress and entrepreneur, once said, "I think the hardest part of aging really is recognizing the time you wasted and the things you worried about that really didn't matter. ... That's really the only regret that I have."

Oprah went on to say that the best part of growing older is being free to do whatever you want to do. "When you combine these two aspects of aging, we realize that aging brings us time and freedom to pursue what is important and the wisdom to know what that is. This is a powerful combination, and when we apply the talents, skills, and perspective, we've gained over a lifetime of experience in that pursuit of what is important to us, we have the power to indulge our passions, fulfill our purpose in life, and change the world—in short, to pursue happiness."

Aging Quality is a Choice

Choices are the hinges of destiny.
— Pythagoras

Let us revisit the two residents of the retirement community in Florida who had polar opposite outlooks towards their remaining years. While one was content to wither away, the other was elated by the prospect of having more time to make a difference in his life and the lives of others. How can there be such a glaring difference in their viewpoints about the quality of their lives in their remaining years?

The quality of our lives is shaped by the quality of our choices. Throughout life, we are faced with opportunities and challenges, and we have choices as to how we respond to each. The culmination of these choices crafts our mindset about the life we have led and how we choose to live going forward. This manifests itself in one of four ways, which are essentially life choices:

- **An Empty Life:** An empty life is one of bitterness and despair, with no sense of optimism or hope for a better future. In this mode, there is no drive or enthusiasm to actively seek gratification or happiness. Many people who have this outlook have no passion. They may view themselves as victims and feel as though they are entitled to the rewards they have not received. People who choose this path are often viewed as complainers, whining about their situations without doing anything to better themselves or improve their lot in life.

- **A Pleasant Life**: People choosing to live a pleasant life often have great passion to participate in activities or acquire belongings that give them great pleasure, and they often pursue these with great zeal. They generally seek immediate gratification from short-lived experiences, whether drinking the finest wines, or driving expensive cars or going on exotic vacations. They will go to any lengths and spend any amount of money to pursue what gives them pleasure.

- **A Good Life:** A good life is one in which the person finds pleasure and gratification in non-monetary ways by using his or her individual talents and strengths to achieve personal satisfaction and accomplish individual goals. People choosing to live a good life generally achieve gratification through accomplishments, as opposed to acquisitions. They tend to focus on specific goals and take specific steps to achieve those goals.

- **A Meaningful Life:** A meaningful life is one with true purpose, which in turn generates abundant gratification and genuine happiness. Martin Seligman, a psychologist and author who is considered the father of positive psychology, describes this concept in one of his books, *Authentic Happiness: The Meaningful Life is Beyond the Good Life*. It consists in attachment to something larger than you. In this mode of life, the larger the entity to which you can attach, the more meaning you will find in your life.

Living a meaningful life means that you move away from your self-centered focus and attach yourself to a cause or purpose that is larger than yourself — and you live your life focused on that cause. In doing so, you create a positive difference in the lives of others and generate authentic and lasting happiness for yourself. A great example of what it means to live a meaningful life can be found in the best-selling book *Being Mortal: Medicine and What Matters in the End*, written by Dr. Atul Gawande, a New England surgeon and author who describes the challenges world-renowned geriatrician Felix Silverstone faced in his final years:

> For Felix Silverstone, a national leader in geriatrics for five decades, managing aging and its distressing realities were the work of a lifetime. He could feel his own mind and body wearing down at age 87. His night vision had become poor. He had begun to lose teeth. He was more concerned about the changes in the brain. What buoyed (sustained) him, despite his limitations, was having a purpose: to be of service, in some way to those around him. He formed a journal-reading club for retired physicians, guided a young geriatrician through her first research study and facilitated a survey of attitudes about aging.

This is a classic example of leading a meaningful life. Rather than complaining about his physical ailments, Mr. Silverstone chose to use his personal experience and knowledge to help others. In choosing to do so, he had a positive impact on the people around him, while achieving happiness and gratification in his own life as well.

Each of us has a choice as to whether to live an Empty Life, a Pleasant Life, a Good Life or a Meaningful Life. Choose wisely.

We Create/Cement a Legacy as We Age

The idea is not to live forever;

it is to create something that will.

— Andy Warhol

"Every five years, for as long as I live, I will write a new book!"

Having experienced personal happiness by sharing my knowledge through writing books, I made the above pledge in the presence of more than 100 family members and friends who attended the celebration for my 75th birthday five years ago. Some of my guests may have thought I was joking, however, those closest to me know this was a public declaration of my commitment to living a meaningful life and creating my legacy.

A person's legacy can come in many forms. Mahatma Gandhi's legacy of nonviolence has inspired generations of leaders around the world, including Martin Luther King, Jr., Nelson Mandela, the Dalai Lama, Aung San Suu Kyi and many others. Mother Teresa's legacy of helping the sick and poor served as a beacon to many. President John F. Kennedy's legacy of taking responsibility for the government and the world continues to inspire countless people to embrace public service.

Is leaving a legacy solely the prerogative of people who are famous or rich? Not at all. Everyone leaves a legacy of some sort. But it's up to me and you decide what each of our legacies will be. In his book *Legacies Aren't Just for Dead People: Discover Happiness and a Meaningful Life by Creating and Enjoying Your Legacies Now*, author Robb Lucy aptly defines a legacy as "something I create that connects and enhances lives now and will continue to positively affect others when I am gone."

Creating our legacy is an innate part of human nature; it generally remains hidden in our subconscious throughout our lives and creeps out as we grow older and approach our senior years. With wisdom acquired over the years, coupled with additional free time generally available later in life, we tend to reflect on how we will be remembered and plan for ways we will construct our legacy.

At the time I made the pronouncement to publish a new book every five years, I had already published my first book, *Organizational Turnarounds with a Human Touch,* in 2011, through which I shared my professional experience and personal advice to help individuals and organizations seeking to rejuvenate their business models. The book had a positive impact on those who read it, as well as the organizations that benefited from it. Based on that experience, I decided that writing books was a way for me to continue to share the knowledge I had acquired throughout my life in a way that would benefit others while also reinforcing my personal legacy. By publicly declaring that I would publish a new book every five years, I also was making a commitment to myself to follow through.

Early in 2017, I published my second book, *Seizing Success: How Mindset Makes It Happen,* which proved to be even more impactful than my first book. It also set me on the path to writing this, my third book, to provide insights and advice on living a meaningful life as we age. In doing so, my commitment to continue writing is intact, and my legacy has started to sprout. Not only am I fulfilling my commitment, but I also am feeling fulfilled and inspired by the process, which enables me to live a meaningful life.

Creating and reinforcing our legacy provides motivation, a sense of mission and tremendous happiness as we age.

If you haven't yet thought about creating your legacy, start now. It's never too late to begin. You may find inspiration in these words of Pablo Picasso: *The meaning of life is to find your gift, and the purpose of life is to give it away.*

Begin by reflecting on your life and trying to identify YOUR purposeful passion — something that provides gratification and happiness for you, while also benefiting others.

Once you have determined a purposeful passion, start mapping out your plan to execute it with discipline and determination. Remember the story of Felix Silverstone who, at age 87, found his passion by using his expertise in geriatrics to mentor others. That is exactly what I did at the age of 75, when I decided to share my expertise by writing books. It also is what my friend in our retirement community did at age 86, when he shared his leadership skills by developing activities and other opportunities to improve the quality of life for other seniors in our community

Identifying, creating and reinforcing your legacy take work. You must focus on the process and not on the results. Draw inspiration and wisdom from these words of an oriental proverb: *He who plants the sweetest tree rarely lives to eat the fruits of that tree, but those who eat, thank the one who planted it and draw inspiration from him to do similar deeds.*

Active Cohorts

Assimilating the gist of our four realities — that aging is a lifelong process; that it is about living and not ceasing to live; that the quality of our aging process is a choice; and that it is essential to use this time to create and/or cement our legacy — helps us realize that aging is not a cruelty of nature, but rather a benediction to fulfill our human existence. That realization has the power of transmuting us from seniors seen as entitled, complaining victims into proactive participants in the aging process, dealing with the challenges and opportunities presented to us in our senior years.

By actively engaging in decision-making about our physical and mental health and by pursuing our passions as we find purpose in our lives, we can become productive contributors in our later years rather than a burden to our families and society. By living a meaningful life, we can help change the negative stereotypes associated with aging and help bring seniors back to the revered status they once held, described by words such as these:

- Wise
- Reflective
- Mentor
- Caring
- Asset
- Cherished

A Balancing Act

There is no denying that growing old is not easy; aging comes with its own issues and challenges. "The story of aging is the story of our parts," Dr. Atul Gawande says in his book, *Being Mortal: Medicine and What Matters in the End.* As we age, our bodily organs, including our brains, degenerate and create serious challenges to our flexibility, memory, dexterity and other aspects of daily functioning. Compounding these issues is the stress many of us feel as society struggles to care for the ever-increasing number of elderly with a finite number of resources.

However, the truth is we also approach the last years of our lives armed with accumulated virtues of hope, purpose, competence, love, caring and, most important, reflection and wisdom. These virtues give us enormous power to deal with our limitations in more effective ways. In other words, our cumulative experiences of reaching the various milestones throughout our lives have also made us wiser and more flexible when it comes to dealing with our limitations. Consider the example of the esteemed painter known as Grandma Moses. When she found she could no longer pursue embroidery as a hobby because of her arthritis, she took up painting instead. Her experience is a classic example of looking beyond limitations to seek and charter new paths to fulfillment.

The bottom line: We do not have to capitulate to physical and mental decline and/or suffering as we age if we can balance this with the creation and/or reinforcement of a personal legacy that uplifts others. Happiness generated by the pursuit of this balance will help diminish our suffering while improving our mental health, providing a sense of contentment in our later years. What is required is a new dynamic mindset that pulls us out of our comfort zone and propels us into an adventurous pursuit of the last milestone of our human existence – creating and cementing a lasting legacy of which we can be proud.

Guided by reflection and powered by wisdom, we enter the final stages of the aging process in quest of the last milestone of life – creating and fortifying our legacy.

Chapter 2

The Power of Our Mindset

Your beliefs become your thoughts,

your thoughts become your words,

your words become your actions,

your actions become your habits,

your habits become your values,

and your values become your destiny.

— Mahatma Gandhi

How come my life is miserable compared with others?

Am I destined to be a failure?

Why does success remain elusive for me?

Why am I the only one in this wretched situation?

If you have never heard or uttered any of the above laments, you must not be living on planet Earth! Since the dawn of civilization, most individuals have blamed fate and their personal circumstances for their unfulfilled dreams. As time marches on, these laments become louder and more frequent, with an increased sense of hopelessness and misery.

Below is a shocking view of the mindset of most people, as described by Barry Ritholtz, founder and chief investment officer of Ritholtz Wealth Management, a financial expert and columnist for Bloomberg Opinion, who also writes books and blogs, hosts radio shows and podcasts, and serves as a guest commentator for CNBC, TheStreet.com and other major news outlets.

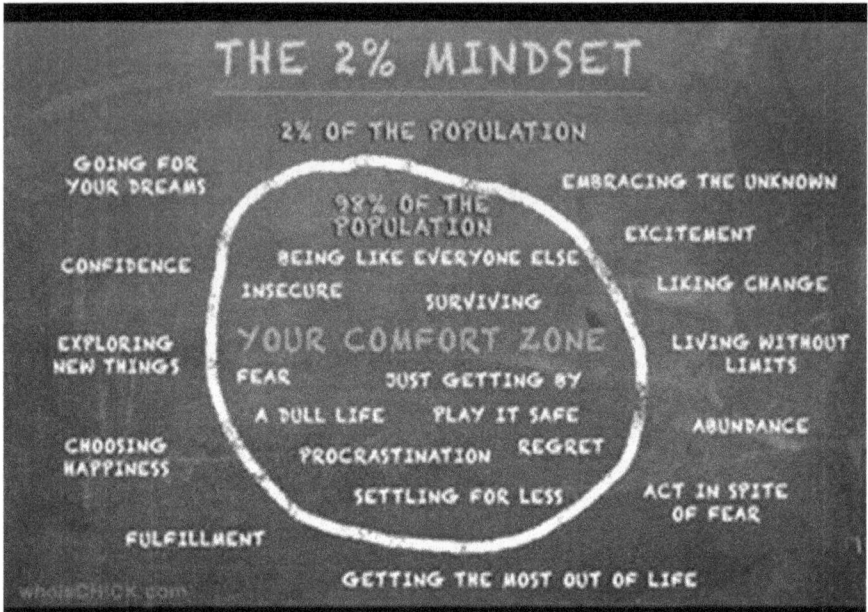

THE 2% MINDSET

2% OF THE POPULATION

GOING FOR
YOUR DREAMS

EMBRACING THE UNKNOWN

98% OF THE
POPULATION

EXCITEMENT

CONFIDENCE

BEING LIKE EVERYONE ELSE

INSECURE   SURVIVING

LIKING CHANGE

EXPLORING
NEW THINGS

YOUR COMFORT ZONE

FEAR   JUST GETTING BY

LIVING WITHOUT
LIMITS

A DULL LIFE   PLAY IT SAFE

CHOOSING
HAPPINESS

PROCRASTINATION   REGRET

ABUNDANCE

SETTLING FOR LESS

ACT IN SPITE
OF FEAR

FULFILLMENT

GETTING THE MOST OUT OF LIFE

wholeCHICK.com

We can debate the preciseness of the percentages shown here, but we can't hide from the simple fact that, for most of us, our mindset can lead to a life marked by insecurity, fear, boredom, inadequacy and despondency. By contrast, only a tiny minority of people have learned to develop a mindset that enables them to see and live their lives positively, with a sense of anticipation, excitement and fulfillment.

Retired seniors are no exception. In my ongoing journey of retirement, I have ample opportunities to interact and discourse with retirees as young as 60 years old as well as those in their early 90s. Despite their sound financial and health status in the early years of their retirement, their mindset about the remaining years of their lives is often quite pessimistic. They have no illusions as to the ultimate end of their lives, but the journey to that finale often seems full of fear and uncertainty. Using the comparison set forth by Barry Ritholtz, here is how I would summarize the general mindset of the elderly:

Elderly World

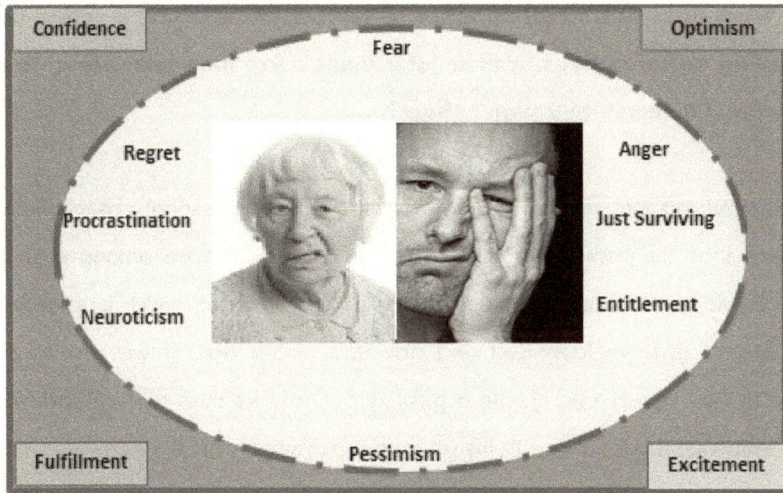

Confidence | Optimism
Fear
Regret | Anger
Procrastination | Just Surviving
Neuroticism | Entitlement
Fulfillment | Pessimism | Excitement

Baldev K Seekri

As with the breakdown for the general population, a large majority of seniors are victims of the wrong mindset — one that is manifested in regret, anger, entitlement and/or insecurity. Those feelings are clearly seen in the following common laments:

Am I destined to suffer in my old age?

Why do I feel lonely, bored and helpless?

Why am I not being taken care of by others?

Why does happiness elude me?

When will this nightmare end?

Just as a minority of the total population has a positive mindset that allows them to lead fulfilling lives, only a small percentage of seniors have found a way to make the last phase of their lives meaningful and joyful.

Rather than dreading the next day, seniors with a positive mindset and outlook look forward to making each new day exciting and challenging.

What does this small minority of seniors know about creating and enjoying fulfilling lives in their later years? Are they just lucky, or do they have a secret they won't share?

Combining the wisdom of many experts and my personal observations, I believe that the answer is neither luck nor a secret shared among a select few. Instead, it's a matter of having the proper mindset, which is something too few of us have identified and adopted as we age. If we wish to join those in the minority and create a positive outlook, we must fully comprehend and embrace the following truths about our personal mindset.

We Are the Product of Our Mindset

> Much of what you think of as your personality actually grows out of your mindset. Much of what may be preventing you from fulfilling your potential grows out of your mindset.
>
> — Carol S. Dweck, author of Mindset:
> The New Psychology of Success

Our mindset is our mental state — our attitude — that is at the heart of how we perceive reality and our place in it. It is our disposition that determines our interpretations and reactions to situations, problems and opportunities. These interpretations and reactions translate into our way of understanding and living our lives.

Our Mindset is Enormously Powerful

Our life is the creation of our mind.
— Buddha

Upon publishing my second book, *Seizing Success: How Mindset Makes It Happen*, in 2017, I sent the first copy to my mentor, Late Dr. Judith M. Bardwick, PhD, a psychologist and author of the international best seller *Danger in the Comfort Zone* and nine other books. Till her demise in 2019 at age 86, Dr. Bardwick was actively writing and sharing her wisdom with others, including me. The following is an excerpt from her reply:

Baldev...

Reading your book stimulated me to write a bit about me.

My purpose and priority in terms of the work I do is to make things right. I'm not sure when this started, but it's been key to what I choose to work on.

When I was a doctoral student and it was time to do a dissertation, I happened to return to reading the works of Dr. Sigmund Freud and he was focusing on the subject of women. NO! The high priest in psychology and psychiatry was writing about women-as-not-men. I was furious. By that time, I had two kids and wanted to shake Freud and his followers and say: You are leading a parade and believe your attire is grand, but I will prove to you that you are stark naked. What we need is a literature of women-as-women and not the losers you write about. That book, The Psychology of Women, was written by me. I held the first graduate seminar on the subject and many of the "students" were faculty.

My passion was driven by anger at this devaluation of a whole gender and I didn't care about being liked or fitting in. I wanted to right a wrong. Righting what's wrong is still my guideline.

— Judy

Dr. Bardwick's belief of needing to right a wrong helped craft her mindset early on. The power of that mindset not only helped enable her to write the first- ever book on the psychology of women, but also became the driving force in her future work, leading to her becoming an iconic author, speaker and consultant for numerous individuals and organizations.

For seniors, rather than succumbing to myths and misinformation about old age, reliance on their time-tested beliefs about life will not only make their struggles of aging more manageable, but this will also will give them optimism and confidence to live meaningfully in the balance of their journey.

We Are Responsible for Our Mindset

We are responsible for what we are,
and whatever we wish ourselves to be,
we have the power to make ourselves.
— Swami Vivekananda, Hindu spiritual leader

Our mindset is shaped by our personal beliefs – including our assumptions, experiences and values – and it determines how we conduct our lives. Assumptions are those things we take for granted and assume to be true. Experiences are events we have personally observed, participated in or lived through. Values are those things we hold dear, including the intrinsic sense of right or wrong formulated at an early age and developed over the years.

For instance, if you value a healthy lifestyle, you may choose to follow certain diets and exercise routines and this becomes part of your mindset for healthy living. However, if you value fine dining, you may care less about the calorie count than you do about the quality and variety of foods offered at various restaurants.

Our Mindset Can and Should Be Dynamic

Once your mindset changes,
everything on the outside will change along with it.
— Steve Maraboli,
motivational speaker and best-selling author

Are we doomed to a specific, inflexible mindset that will dictate our entire life? No! Although our beliefs may be strong and deep-rooted, they are not set in concrete. Beliefs are the product/result/outgrowth of our assumptions, experiences and values. Each of these can change over time. As we continue to acquire new experiences and knowledge, we can alter our beliefs and adopt a new mindset. Let us consider the following true case of a reshaped mindset.

At the midpoint of my management career at Texas Instruments in the late 1980s, I was promoted to the position of operations manager for a manufacturing business called PTC that produced precision electronic ceramics. Those components were supplied to some of the worldwide business units of Texas Instruments, which in turn packaged them into devices that were sold to global customers in automotive, industrial, aircraft and other consumer markets. Although it was an internal supplier for the company's other businesses, PTC had to be profitable and stay competitive with external suppliers worldwide in order to survive.

In general, PTC was faring rather well. However, one of its clients, a Texas Instruments business unit in Holland, was constantly threatening to purchase components from an external provider instead of PTC. So, one of the first challenges I faced in my new job was to identify and resolve the issues between PTC and that particular business unit. Accordingly, I called the manufacturing superintendent of PTC to ask why our performance was unacceptable and to solicit his thoughts about resolving the issue. He quickly and firmly replied: "There is no need to waste our time discussing this. It's mission impossible. We will be better off if we focus our efforts on other customers."

Surprised by his response, I asked why he was refusing to address the issue. "No matter what we do, they are not going to be satisfied because they want to buy these parts from European suppliers," he said. "So why waste time trying to get them to buy from PTC instead?"

Over the next two weeks, I spoke with several other people at PTC and got the same answer. It seemed the mindset of the entire organization was fixated on the same assumption: *Europeans will only buy European-made products*. Bizarre as it seemed to me, that was their belief and no one seemed willing to budge from that particular mindset.

Still, this was hard for me to digest. My professional experience did not corroborate that belief. Sure, in every organization there are always a few people who are highly biased towards doing business with specific individuals or companies, but the notion that an entire organization had such a mindset was beyond me.

I decided to challenge that mindset by going to Holland to personally meet with the management team of the business unit there. When I told my staff about my plans, they predicted the trip would be futile; that it was sure to end in humiliation for both me and PTC.

I prepared by making sure I thoroughly understood the strengths and limitations of our manufacturing process, as well as the Holland business unit's requirements in terms of quality, cost and service. Finally, I embarked on the journey to the Texas Instruments plant in Almelo, Holland, which is about 200 miles northwest of Amsterdam.

Upon arrival, I was treated with the obligatory civility expected by our company, but the mood was extremely cold and formal. Those who attended the first meeting made it clear they were there only to listen to what I had to say, but they exhibited no desire to have any meaningful interaction. Reminding myself of the importance of my mission, I made every possible attempt to convey my sincere desire to learn from them and find a way for PTC to meet their needs.

After two days, the environment of mistrust started to change, and signs of collaboration started to surface. More people from higher levels within the Holland business unit started to attend the meetings and they offered their suggestions. In the ensuing days, I explained in depth the strengths and technological limitations of our manufacturing process. In return, they provided me with more specific information about the needs of their automotive customers. By the end of my weeklong visit, we worked together to come up with a plan: we agreed to revise certain specifications for better control of our manufacturing process and established specific mutual goals for improvement on both ends.

On the night before my return to the United States, Gerry Bekkers, the vice president of the Texas Instruments business unit in Holland, joined us for a farewell dinner. He thanked me for coming and said it was the first time their business unit felt like it was being treated like an actual customer and not simply a nuisance.

News of the transformed mindset was music to my ears. Throughout the week, I had seen no evidence to support the notion that the Holland business unit only wanted to buy products from European companies. They simply wanted to buy from a supplier who understood and responded to their needs. On my return to the United States, it took quite a while for the employees at PTC to discard their mindset, which was based on incorrect assumptions, but it eventually happened. Over time, PTC became the preferred supplier for the business unit in Holland, resulting in higher growth and profitability for both of our businesses.

The above example is testimony to the fact that individuals and organizations alike can gain tremendously by constantly examining and challenging long-held beliefs, which results in a dynamic mindset.

Being willing to adjust my personal mindset has helped me throughout the years. My efforts to keep my mindset dynamic by constantly testing my beliefs were a key element of my success in adapting to various challenges and opportunities in my personal and professional life. This process continues even now, and it has been instrumental in making the journey into the final phase of my life more meaningful.

We Can and Should Refine Our Mindset

> To change your life, you have to change yourself.
> To change yourself, you have to change your mindset.
> — Wilson Kanadi, an inspirational writer

We don't need to simply wait for some unexpected event to jolt our beliefs and reshape our mindset. We need the humility to accept that our mindset is not static; it can and must evolve. We must be open to constant learning to substantiate or refute our current beliefs. We must be humble enough to acknowledge that sometimes even our most strongly held beliefs can – or even must – change. Without a true awareness of who we really are and an acceptance of the facts of our reality, we may be more inclined to stick with our current beliefs and not be curious enough to substantiate or refute them.

While humility helps us to see the genuine reality of our mindset, it is our receptivity to learning that makes the transformation of our mindset possible. Learning is a linchpin, without which progress is not only difficult but also often impossible. As the late Dr. Benjamin Barber, a renowned political theorist and best-selling author, once said: "I don't divide the world into the weak and the strong, or the successes and the failures, those who make it or those who don't. I divide the world into learners and non-learners."

In researching this and other books, I have found no better example of humility and openness for learning than the Dalai Lama, the international avatar of compassion and happiness. Even he recognizes the importance of learning and adapting to keep a dynamic mindset, as seen when a reporter questioned his beliefs about the importance of meditation.

The process of meditation, loathed by some as so-called hippie madness or the propaganda of yellow-robed Eastern mystics, is spreading rapidly in the Western world as more people see the physical and emotional benefit of meditation for their bodies and minds. It also is gaining increasing validity in the scientific community, with more funding being allocated to researching the practice of meditation.

A few years ago, a meeting of renowned scientists took place at Emory University in Atlanta, GA, to review ongoing research into meditation and its impact on the human mind and body. One of the invited guests was the Dalai Lama, who also is a staunch supporter of scientific research into meditation. Prior to the meeting, Dan Harris, co-anchor of

ABC'S *Nightline*, had a brief dialogue with the Dalai Lama, which he describes in his best-selling book *10% Happier: How I Tamed the Voice in My Head, Reduced Stress Without Losing My Edge and Found Self-Help That Actually Works*. Mr. Harris asked whether the Dalai Lama was concerned about the possibility that scientific research could debunk his long-held beliefs about meditation?

> **Dan Harris:** *There is a risk. What if scientists discover something that contradicts your faith?*
>
> **Dalai Lama:** *No—no risk. If a scientist confirms nonexistence of something we believe, then we have to accept it.*
>
> **Dan Harris:** *So, if scientists come up with something that contradicts your beliefs, you will change your beliefs?*
>
> **Dalai Lama:** *Oh yes. Yes.*

The reporter was essentially suggesting that the Dalai Lama's entire reputation could be wiped away with a scientific finding that contradicts his beliefs on compassion and meditation. Rather than being afraid of the question or defensive in his response, the Dalai Lama said he openly supports scientific research, even if it might prove him wrong. This demonstrates the Dalai Lama's humility and openness to learning, showing his willingness to refine his mindset and keep it dynamic.

Here's a question for you: When was the last time you challenged and reshaped your mindset by scrutinizing your beliefs, your current reality and your latest learning?

Most people probably can't answer that question. The same can be said for most of the struggling seniors I have encountered during the journey of my retirement. Rather than challenging their long-held beliefs, they stubbornly defend their existing mindset by justifying their current beliefs and clinging to outdated habits, experiences and values. No wonder so many of them find themselves caught in a whirlpool of misery and hopelessness.

Our mindset is shaped by our beliefs, and the quality of our mindset will determine the quality of our aging.

As individuals, we deserve a purposeful and joyful journey during the last chapter of our lives. It is within our power to have that positive experience, provided we understand the superb power of our mindset. We can cling to a mindset based on past values, experiences and beliefs, even if it leaves us feeling hollow and unfulfilled, or we can acknowledge that our mindset must be continually reconfigured and reinvigorated by testing our beliefs, challenging our reality and gaining wisdom, which creates a positive attitude and outlook as we approach each new day. **The choice is ours.**

Chapter 3

The Dynamic Mindset of Aging

A belief is not merely an idea the mind possesses;

it is an idea that possesses the mind.

— Robert Bolton,

communications consultant and author

"I wish I'd had the courage to live a life true to myself, not the life others expected of me."

The above statement is the single biggest regret of people who are dying, according to Bronnie Ware, a palliative care nurse and author of the best-selling memoir *The Five Regrets of the Dying*. Ms. Ware, a native of Australia, spent more than 15 years taking care of people in the final days and weeks of their lives. Based on her interactions with her patients, she learned that most people don't regret not making more money or not having better health. Rather, they regret living with the wrong beliefs about personal fulfillment. That's how she came up with the top five regrets of the dying listed in her book, which lists the other four as:

"I wish I had let myself be happier."

"I wish I had the courage to express my feelings."

"I wish I hadn't worked so hard."

"I wish I had stayed in touch with my friends."

These regrets at the end of life are a strong testament to the fact that most of us spend our entire lives pursuing pseudo contentment, which is much different than the real thing. By the time we realize we have the wrong mindset when it comes to finding true contentment, it is generally too late.

You may think that once people transition into retirement, they are content with their past achievements and choices and express no regrets until they reach their deathbeds. But the reality is far from this assumption. During the 15 years since my retirement, I have had ample opportunity to talk to retired seniors, most of whom admit they have regrets about their pre-retirement lives. Among their regrets:

- Not having had the courage to choose their own career paths, or spending much of their working lives at a job they didn't love;
- Sacrificing time with family members and close friends in order to advance their careers; and
- Not pursuing their passions to experience genuine happiness.

Sadly, even after retiring, many people do nothing to address their past regrets. For example, some of the retirees told me that they had always wanted to write a book or create a memoir of their lives, but they never had time because of their hectic work schedule. Others said they had always wanted to take up painting, or learn a new language, or perfect their music skills or even exercise regularly, but they never had the time. But even now that they have the time to pursue these passions, many lack the motivation or will to do so, so their regrets remain intact.

Why is that so? Why do so many retirees continue procrastinating, carrying their regrets until their last moments on earth? From what I've seen and heard from so many of these retirees over the years, I've come to the conclusion that they are prisoners of their own negative mindset, based on their past experiences and beliefs.

To avoid this pitfall, regardless of where we are in our lives, we must acknowledge the power of our mindset — and believe that we have the pow-

er to change our mindset at any time. We can choose to do nothing and continue to live with regrets, or we can make a conscious effort to create a positive mindset based on the things we want to do and the lives we want to lead. Remember: aging is the process of living, not ceasing to live, and we all have the choice of living meaningful lives as we age.

For all seniors: Remember that at this point in your life, as you approach the final milestone, you should focus on creating and fortifying your legacy, not ruminating about regrets. You must acknowledge and accept that your mindset controls your quality of life, right up until the end. So, if you want to approach your final years with a positive attitude and outlook, continuing to achieve personal goals and contribute to your community, you must take charge of your mindset and make the necessary changes to get you there.

The following chart compares two extremes of potential mindsets: classic and dynamic. The Classic Mindset of aging, which many of us have, often leaves us chasing a vision of fulfilment that is more like a mirage; something we think we want but likely can never attain. The Dynamic Mindset, on the other hand, focuses on the realities of meaningful aging and allows us to achieve contentment in its truest form.

The Classic Mindset is built on beliefs that are suppositions not supported by personal experience or other evidence and often based in ignorance. The Dynamic Mindset is built on beliefs driven by the realities of aging combined with a desire to change one's mindset to focus on things that are important to you and will bring you genuine fulfillment in the final stages of life.

Aging Mindset Choices

Classic Mindset	Dynamic Mindset
. Continual Nightmare.	. Essential Quest.
. Aging quality is encoded by my fate.	. Aging quality is sculpted with my efforts.
. Others must take care of me.	Personal responsibility to make aging meaningful.
. Nothing Left to learn and accomplish.	. Continuous Learning is the soul of worthwhile aging.
. Passion(s) is adequate for good aging.	. Purposeful passion(s) is vital for meaningful aging.

Baldev K Seekri

In the following five chapters, we will focus on the Dynamic Mindset, which creates the best opportunity to allow us to achieve true fulfillment in our final years. You will learn how to adapt each of these elements as integral parts of your own Dynamic Mindset. We also will examine the experiences of five seniors who have achieved fulfilment in their personal and professional lives before and even after retiring. They serve as living proof of the validity of each element of this archetypal mindset. Let me introduce them to you now:

- **Dr. Paul James Maryan, PhD:** Born in England and now living in the Philippines, Dr. Mayan is 72 years old and views life as an ongoing string of events that are part of his quest for living life with a larger purpose focused on giving — not giving up. Dr. Paul's life is a great testimony to the fact that meaningful aging is an essential quest rather than the dreaded nightmare envisioned by many seniors.

- **Air Marshall S. Raghavendran:** A native of India now living in the United States, Marshall Raghavendran was formerly Vice Chair of Air Staff for the Indian Air Force. Now 90 years old, he exemplifies the importance of having a dynamic mindset that focuses on achieving a high quality of life at all ages. His life story before and after his retirement gives credence to the fact that it is within our power to shape the quality of our life at any age, rather than capitulating to limitations and myths of our fate.

- **Dolores Cummins:** Born in Ireland and now living in Australia, Ms. Cummins is a strategic adviser, corporate educator and author. She learned the importance of personal responsibility as a young woman, reflecting on life while mourning the tragedy of his first-born's death. That new belief of taking personal responsibility transformed a shy and dependent young woman into a person capable of living life with courage, integrity and purpose. Ms. Cummins, who is approaching age 60, shares her thoughts about how taking personal responsibility helped her throughout her life and how she intends to use that mindset when she enters her golden years.

- **Vishwakant Mankodi:** At 87 years old, Mr. Mankodi, a successful businessman in his pre-retirement life and a musician at heart, who continues to perfect his skills in singing melodies on harmonium. Born in India and having settled in the United States for the past 50 years, Mr. Mankodi personifies the power of a dynamic mindset for continual learning. His refusal to let age interfere with his quest for learning can serve as great inspiration to those seniors whose mindset includes the fallacious belief that learning becomes impossible later in life.

- **Mai Donohue:** A writer and self-taught cook, Ms. Donohue is a retired educator of special needs students. At a very young age, she beat all odds to escape from Vietnam in 1970 and settled in Rhode Island, United States. In retirement, Ms. Donohue has combined her passions for writing and home cooking with a larger purpose to help needy students. Ms. Donohue embodies the notion that a dynamic mindset requires there must be a purpose aligned passion(s).

Chapter 4

Aging — An Essential Quest

It takes a long time to become young.

— Pablo Picasso

Dr. Paul Maryan, PhD

Palawan Island in the Philippines

What does aging mean to you?

"It's another stamp in my passport for the ongoing journey of my life."

What role does learning play in your life?

"Life is a continuous learning process so that you can use your knowledge for the betterment of those around you."

What have you learned the most as you age?

"Recognizing that finishing well outweighs starting well and failing badly."

The above responses of Dr. Paul Maryan to a questionnaire I created to identify credible case studies to support my theories on the importance of mindset during aging were breaths of fresh air compared to the outright despair I recently felt when discussing the aging process with some of my close friends.

I have long believed in the importance of using our final years to create or cement our legacy, especially when it comes to using our experience and knowledge to benefit others. But some of my friends scoff at the very notion. "What difference does a legacy mean once we are dead?" one friend retorted, adding that leaving a legacy means nothing to him since he will not be around to experience its impact.

"But it could make a difference for someone else," I said.

I shared with him the parable of a young child who comes upon a beach littered with starfish that had been washed ashore by the high tide. Realizing the starfish would die if left out in the sun, he began throwing them back in the water, one by one. "What are you doing?" a passerby asked. "Saving the starfish," the child replied. The passerby questioned what difference it made, since the child couldn't possibly save them all. The child picked up another starfish and tossed it into the water, saying: "Well, I made a difference for that one."

My story failed to sway my friend's opinion. He insisted that we must enjoy the remaining period of our lives without worrying about creating a legacy that we can't experience after we die. My other friends said nothing, and the conversation instead turned to concerns about finances and death. We then agreed the subject of aging was too sad to discuss, so the conversation ended there.

MEANINGFUL AGING

In stark contrast to the lives of many of my affluent friends, Dr. Maryan's life has been a constant struggle. Yet, still he continues to be enthusiastic about his ongoing life journey and treats every day of his life as another date on his passport he is carrying for his ongoing journey. Inspired by his mindset of embracing aging, rather than despising or fearing it as many people do, I asked Dr. Maryan to share his life experiences and how he came to achieve such a positive attitude.

At age 72, Dr. Maryan currently lives on a farm on the island of Palawan in the Philippines, with his wife Beth and two of her sons, both of whom have autism. With his assistance, both of the boys are able to work on the farm and achieve enough success in their tasks to feel independent. In addition to helping the boys and managing the farm, Dr. Maryan has established a consultancy business, Activatek PI Corp., and he assists the Philippine Department of Trade and Industry in training local business leaders to develop sound business management skills, such as decision-making, marketing, branding and leadership. With a master's degree in marketing, his wife Beth Maryan also pitches in to help local businesses. Meanwhile, the couple is also venturing into producing and marketing organic food at their farm. They are barely making ends meet, but they are always willing to mentor and help others.

Despite the challenges he has faced and the struggles he has endured throughout his life, Dr. Maryan has created a positive mindset that enables him to give back instead of giving up. He credits this positive mindset to his upbringing and life experiences, which he shares with us here:

I was born in England and immigrated to the United States at the age of 16 months. My father had served in the Army in Palestine and my mother was an ambulance driver in London during the blitz. My life in the USA provided no good memories; my mother

45

suffered a mental breakdown, which resulted in a very difficult life for my dad and my future siblings. We relocated back to the United Kingdom after some 10 years of living in the United States, and we restarted our family life in England.

I was the eldest of five children and had the responsibility of taking care of my brothers and sisters, as my mother's health only worsened over the years. With all this constant upheaval in my own life, my education and personal life were secondary to helping my mother and my siblings.

I started working at age 16 to support my family. I began by working in a friend's family business as a trainee for a few years, and then joined S&H Green Stamps as a salesman. That was my first entry into sales management. My hard work and compassion for others earned me the respect and admiration of my boss, Mr. David Coren, the managing director of the organization, and soon I was promoted to the position of regional sales manager.

After Mr. Coren left the organization to become the managing director of another company, the Heron Organization, he approached me to join him there as a general manager of one of the newly acquired motor dealerships in Birmingham. That would serve to be my first step into the world of the automotive industry.

I spent the next 35 years in the automotive industry, working hard, earning promotions and praises, and helping others along the way. Due to moving around since my early childhood (from the UK to the USA and back to the UK) and taking responsibility for my family, my education was a mess. I had always loved reading and had a desire for higher education, but lacked the resources and time to pursue a higher degree due to family commitments.

One of our customers, a general manager for a Mercedes Benz importer, had enrolled in an online MBA program with the University of Liverpool. I decided to join that program in 2009 and, three years later, after many hours of study, giving up my weekends and personal life, I earned my MBA with top grades. I was overwhelmed with this accomplishment, especially after so many years of feeling disadvantaged. It proved there are no real limits when it comes to learning, regardless of your age.

Earning my MBA changed my attitude as to the importance of all business leaders pursuing degrees in higher education. What I learned opened my eyes to new business management techniques to which I had not previously been exposed. It was truly an awesome experience. I also became a born-again Christian in 2006, recognizing the need to have a true God in my life.

I retired from the automotive industry in 2011 at age 65 as the chief operating officer of Nasser Bin Khaled (NBK) in Qatar, having covered the markets of Abu Dhabi, Dubai, Bahrain, Jordan and Qatar.

My decision to retire at age 65 was primarily driven by a restructuring of the NBK group, prompting me to consider a change for my future.

Keeping a clear focus on my values of giving but not giving up, I was now ready to welcome the next stamp on our passport of life. Based on the recommendations of a longtime friend, Beth and I decided to move to Paphos, Cyprus, which we saw as a stepping stone into the future — wherever that was going to take us. We went on to set up a consulting business in Paphos.

Soon after our arrival there in 2012, the Greek banking crisis hit Europe, which had a major impact on Cyprus. This was a catastrophic event, with banks closing for days, restrictions imposed on cash withdrawals and much calamity for local businesses.

Unicars, a large family group in the used car business, approached me out of the blue, asking me and Beth to work for them on a month-to-month basis, working on small business-related projects covering operations and marketing. But I didn't really see any opportunity to grow and help others in that fragmented market.

Meanwhile, Beth and I also had married in July 2012 and, later that year, we travelled to Manila, Philippines, to celebrate the 70th birthday of Beth's mother. We also visited Palawan, where her parents had substantial land and farm interests.

The trip proved to be eventful, as that's where I met Irene, a longtime friend and colleague of Beth, who headed a local mission for tribal children, through which she supported their personal ambitions. My mindset of giving and helping others kicked in and I felt a strong yearning to get involved and support Irene in her humanitarian work, so I purchased a motor bike and side car so I could assist her with her program. It was a sizable personal investment of nearly 100,000 pesos (about $5,500) for us.

In the Philippines, Palawan is an incredibly beautiful island with natural seascapes and landscapes; it is one of the most biodiverse of the islands there. Palawan claimed the top spot, based on over 76,000 votes, in Conde Nast Traveler's Readers' Choice Awards for 2014. Beth's father had started farming there more than 25 years ago, investing in mango trees to generate future income. Over time, he had acquired considerable land investments, including the farm where we now live. However, not long ago, the mango trees became infected, thus leaving the farm without any income.

A strong desire to help Beth's parents in the beautiful and peaceful environments of the Island, combined with our stagnant life in Cyprus, made us choose Palawan as our next stop in our ongoing journey. We decided to move to Palawan to help revitalize the land, encourage Beth's boys to become independent and help the locals, including Irene's tribal mission.

Also, the sudden parting with NBK prompted me to enroll in a five-year doctoral program at the Louisiana Baptist University and Seminary in Shreveport, LA. It was an online graduate program for passionate Christian Bible students. I did not want another business degree, so the prospect of undertaking an inspirational program built around a Christian leadership strategy appealed to me. I received my PhD in Communication, Leadership and Governance in 2018 at age 71, and it felt great to realize that aging is not a barrier to learning and relentlessly seeking knowledge for the betterment of self and others.

We continue our lives here in Palawan, cognizant of the fact that this stay is temporary and we need to be ready for the next stop, whenever and wherever the journey of our lives takes us. But one thing is constant: we will continue to strive to give back and not give up, and we will always keep our key belief in the forefront, which is that that finishing well outweighs starting well and failing badly.

Valuable lessons from Dr. Maryan's life: Dr. Maryan has created an exceptional mindset in that he continues to view aging as an essential quest rather than an uninspired march to the end of life.

Dr. Mayan's life experiences underscore the fact that perceptions shape our reality, a topic I explored in detail in my manifesto, *How Per-*

ceptions Shape Realities, published in 2012. As we go through this journey we call life, many of us don't realize that each of our life experiences along the way shapes our reality —and, by extension, our mindset. Some people undertake this journey as a task to be endured, just waiting for it to end. This leads to a meaningless life. But if we view the journey as an adventure, filled with opportunities to learn and experience new things and meaningful purpose, this will lead to self-satisfaction and increased self-esteem. This inspiring view of our journey through life is powered by both our mind and our heart. The net result is a feeling of success and happiness as we enter the final phase of our lives.

Although my previous manifesto was written for business professionals, as a guide to help them achieve success and happiness in their professional and personal lives, the content is equally, if not more relevant, to seniors. Our perceptions of life's journey will help establish our mindset and our outlook towards our remaining years. This in turn will dictate the quality of our lives and the legacy we will leave behind.

We have a choice. If we choose to believe that aging is a forced trip and futile journey to the end, our final years will be miserable and unbearable. However, if we choose to believe that these are the golden years, we will see the journey as a quest with meaningful purpose. This will help us approach the final phase of our lives with enthusiasm and resiliency as we pursue a meaningful goal that is ambitious, fervent, benevolent and joyful. Choosing this path will help us to live our remaining years with positive anticipation instead of merely existing in misery.

Dr. Maryan is among those who believe that the ongoing journey of life is a meaningful quest and not just a meaningless path to the end. While his mindset of giving and not giving up was formed when he was a young man dealing with adversities, every choice he had made in subsequent years has reinforced that mindset. Continually learning, including earning his MBA and PhD in later years, he believes in bettering himself to help others. He also continues to embrace every opportunity to serve his family and his community, helping ensure that his life journey is indeed a meaningful quest.

Through his mindful commitment and heartfelt devotion to excel in hard times and help others, Dr. Maryan has found the secret of meaningful aging: believing and demonstrating that we can achieve true happiness in the last phase of our life through service to others. Exploring and pursuing purposes that are larger than ourselves not only creates our legacy, but also serves as a source of genuine contentment that we truly deserve. Dr. Maryan's commitment to help others brings to mind this quote:

I slept and I dreamed that life is all joy.
I woke and saw that life is all service.
I served and I saw that service is joy.
— Kahlil Gibran

Chapter 5

Aging Quality is Sculpted

Retired Air Marshal S. Raghavendran

Indian Air Force

In the first chapter of this book, I mentioned a 90-year-old resident of my retirement community in Florida who was committed to improving the quality of life for his fellow residents by creating a variety of interactive activities, from book discussion groups to improving facilities. That man, who has found joy in his senior years by making a difference in the lives of others, is Air Marshal S. Raghavendran, a highly decorated pilot who served for more than four decades with the Indian Air Force, retiring in 1988 as Vice Chief of the Air Staff.

Air Marshal Raghavendran, affectionately called Raghu by his staff and friends alike, joined the Indian Air Force at a historic time – within a month after India declared its independence from Great Britain in 1947. He was barely 17 years old, the minimum age for joining the Royal Indian Air Force, as it was called back then. That was the start of a career that spanned 41 years. Over the years, he earned respect as a combat leader – twice commanding fighter squadrons, including one that fought during the India-Pakistan War in 1965. During his rise to the rank of Air Marshal, he was awarded the Ati Vishisht Seva Medal, a prestigious presidential award for "distinguished service of an exceptional order," for his exemplary service and the Param Vishisht Seva Medal for exceptional peacetime service in recognition of his contributions to the operational preparedness of the Indian Air Force before he retired in 1988.

I met Marshal Raghavendran in 2015 when we spent our first winter in the retirement community where Raghu and his family have spent their winters since 2014. I was immediately impressed by his zest for life and his commitment to creating an inviting and engaging environment for his fellow seniors, but I was also curious as to why he was so focused on reaching out to helping others when so many people his age tend to focus on themselves, seeking peace in seclusion.

So, I decided to try to get to know him better, in large part to understand his mindset about aging. I joined his discussion group and supported his efforts to perpetuate engagement and involvement among our fellow residents. Over time, as we worked together to promote and facilitate his ideas and initiatives, we became trusted companions in carrying out his mission to improve our community for all who lived there. Watching this man, who once served as second-in-command of the fourth largest Air Force in the world, patiently teaching other seniors how to safely exercise by riding bicycles was truly inspirational.

MEANINGFUL AGING

As our mutual respect and admiration grew, Raghu mentioned that he had written two memoirs about his career with the Indian Air Force. The first book, *Panther Red One: Memoirs of a Fighter Pilot*, covered his life as a pilot, and his second book, *Panther Red One — The Sequel*, covered his administrative and leadership assignments as a commander.

After reading both books, I was amazed by his perseverance throughout his career, achieving a level of excellence in each assignment he undertook. However, what inspired me the most was his humility; he considered his achievements and successes as ordinary and routine.

In a note he sent to me after I complimented him about his books, he wrote: "It never struck me that I was doing something extraordinary or different from what most others would do." He acknowledged getting some "plum jobs" during his career, but downplayed his accomplishments and the tremendous recognition he had received, saying only that he had "picked up a couple of medals along the way."

As those who know him personally or by reading his books can attest, Raghu's career is truly extraordinary. He earned a reputation for dramatically improving suboptimal situations, systems and procedures by identifying and implementing creative modifications and solutions. One of his many successes was transforming the substandard training program and procedures he encountered when he was assigned to the Indian Air Force's Headquarters Training Command in Bangalore, now known as Bengaluru, in Southern India. He was 45 at the time and had already been promoted to the rank of Air Commodore and Senior Air Staff Officer. In his book, *Panther Red One — The Sequel*, he recalls his initial impressions of that assignment:

I arrived there with a mindset that this was a cushy job with well-oiled training institutions churning out officers and men of every trade, and (thought) all I had to do was to relax and watch it happen.

By the time I finished my first round of visits to all the flying, technical and administrative training units, I was a shaken man. There were many classes for the airmen where there were neither desks nor chairs. They sat on the ground and the desks were their laps. For drill purposes, there weren't even enough dummy wooden rifles to go around. When I asked about the lesson plans and the training aids, I was met with a blank stare!

He immediately ordered an assessment of all aspects of the program, from the furniture and equipment to training protocols. Using his status as senior officer, he ordered the staff to take the necessary steps to bring the facilities and training program up to current standards. Given that most of the focus there was on flight instruction, he dedicated his attention to improving the technical and administrative aspects of the training.

Working with a team of other officers, he helped create the first-ever set of standardized instructions, called the Training Command Air Staff Instructions (TCASI), which superseded any previous instructional guidelines. He also ordered the necessary parts for hands-on training in aircraft maintenance and repair, something the unit had never had before. **The work he was doing was so critical that he was barely given time off to attend funeral services for his mother.** However, he so impressed the Commander-in-Chief, Air Vice Marshal G.K. John, that the marshal recommended Raghu for the Ati Vishisht Seva Medal, which he was subsequently awarded in 1976.

That's just one example from Raghu's exemplary career that demonstrated his commitment to moving beyond the status quo. He refused to accept the substandard situation as it was and instead analyzed the current state of affairs, identified the strengths and weaknesses, and proposed improvements that benefited everyone at Headquarters Training Command and the Indian Air Force, as well.

Raghu took the same approach with our retirement community, seeing the potential for improvement in the conditions there. He identified the need to create shared physical and intellectual activities for the residents who lived there and then programs designed to satisfy those needs to create a more stimulating environment for us all.

What a striking parallel! Reading Raghu's successful turnaround of the Indian Air Force's Headquarters Training Command facilities and training system, his indispensability for his superiors, and his subsequent recognition by earning the Ati Vishisht Seva Medal pulled me back into memory lane in terms of my own professional career. Although I didn't orchestrate any great marvel like Raghu did to win the prestigious Ati Vishisht Medal from the government, nevertheless, my accomplishment described below at a very young age of 26 reflected a very similar mindset as that of Raghu when it came to transforming a situation riddled with chronic problems into a model of excellence.

In 1965, at age 25, I was hired by an Indo-Japanese company named Indoberg in Calcutta, now known as Kolkata, India. Six months after starting my job, I received a call from S.C. Jain, then vice-president of the company, advising me to take the first available flight to join him in Trichy, approximately 200 miles south of Madras, which is now called Chenai, India. Mr. Jain had gone there to visit with the management of Bharat Heavy Electrical (BHL), a major energy production unit of the Indian government and a key customer of our company. However, I had no idea why I was being summoned there to join him in such a hurry. At that time, I had never even flown in an airplane, which further added to my apprehension.

When I arrived in Trichy, I was met by Mr. Jain, who informed me that I was being assigned to replace the resident engineer who was currently there, and I would assume responsibility for overseeing a large ongoing project to the satisfaction of BHL management. He promised me his full support and any necessary resources to carry out that critical project.

At that time in my life, it seemed as I was being tossed into a hornet's nest! For a moment, I started to doubt my own sanity.

After getting over the initial shock of being assigned to such an important task at that stage in my young life, I started to look at the situation objectively and viewed it as a challenge. The morale of the entire team of engineers and skilled craftsmen assigned to the project in Trichy was extremely low, and they seemed resigned to the fact that the project was doomed to fail. I quickly realized that If I didn't take charge and streamline the execution of this project quickly, BHL was likely to cancel its contract and file a lawsuit against our company because of the potential for significant harm to the Indian government if this project was not properly carried out.

I had no choice but to roll my sleeves and get to work. Mustering courage, and using the authority Mr. Jain had vested in me, I devoted all of my energy into making drastic changes to the execution of the project, which included bulldozing barriers – many of which were inflicted by the previous project manager. Soon after taking charge, I saw a glimmer of hope that the project could be saved.

Rather than offering excuses for our poor past performance, I humbly apologized to BHL's management and promised them a swift turnaround. I pledged that my team would work around the clock and provide frequent updates as to our progress for their review and suggestions. In less than six months, the project was not only on track, but it also was forecasted for completion two months ahead of the date specified in the contract. Thanks to the hard work of our entire team, we were able to transform BHL's complaints into complimentary letters to Mr. Jain.

MEANINGFUL AGING

At the time I was assigned to the BHL project in Trichy, I was making plans to marry my wife-to-be, Kamlesh. In fact, my parents had set the date for the ceremony and had already invited the guests. **When I asked for two weeks off for my wedding, I was stunned when Mr. Jain denied my request, saying he couldn't afford to spare me from the project for even a single day.** But I knew that if the wedding did not go off as planned, we would have to postpone the ceremony for nine months, until the next sacred date, per Hindu tradition. So, after a sleepless night, I made the decision to ignore Mr. Jain's denial of my request for time off and I flew home for my wedding. I asked one of my assistants to let Mr. Jain know where I was and to tell him that I would be back a week later, with my new bride.

I was terrified to return to work after taking the unauthorized time off, convinced that I would be fired. But upon our return to Trichy, to my surprise and relief, Mr. Jain met us at the airport with flower garlands. Instead of being fired, I was given a hefty raise and commendations for my performance with BHL to that point. The project was completed 18 months later, well ahead of schedule, and the Indian government was so pleased with our performance that it awarded additional business to our company in the nearby southern state of Andhra Pradesh. I became the resident engineer for that new business and successfully completed that project in two and a half years. On my return to Calcutta, I was promoted to the position of works manager, or plant manager, at age 29. Little did I know that would be my prelude to managing many large businesses in the United States years later.

As with Raghu, my career also was filled with challenges requiring fast turnarounds of situations at companies in the United States as well as other countries. The last assignment before my retirement in 2005 required the turnaround of one of Texas Instruments' business units in Aguascalientes, Mexico. That business, which employed thousands of employees and had a large operating budget, was in a dire situation due to deteriorating profitability and pitiable customer service. It required two and a half years of hard work to transform that operation to a high-performing standard. My wife and I had to move to Mexico, where we lived from 2002 to 2005, to achieve success with that project. The dedicated efforts of the entire team saved the business from closing down, thus protecting the employment of thousands of employees who worked there.

A Fateful Unification: The mighty hand of destiny brought Raghu and me together in the Shantiniketan Retirement Community in Tavares, Florida, to use our abilities to sculpt improvements in various situations to enhance the quality of life for our fellow residents. Each of us had separately spent our lives sculpting situations and systems to advance our careers to the pinnacle of success; now we had come together to make a positive difference in the lives of others – and we are not stopping now.

Even at our age, with Raghu now 90 and me now 80, we are constantly looking for ways to make life more meaningful and dignified for everyone in our community. Whereas Raghu is persistently highlighting and challenging sub-optimal practices and policies, I am busy sharing with our fellow residents what I have learned about meaningful aging.

What differentiates Raghu and me from the multitude of seniors who succumb to the frailties and limitations of their advancing years, idly waiting for the last curtain to fall?

The answer is simple: Each of us has a dynamic mindset based upon the belief that, despite the limitations of our physical circumstances, we can sculpt a better quality of life for ourselves and others. Our lifelong personal and professional achievements, as well as our commitment to helping others, are a testimony to this belief. Our mindset of sculpting a better quality of life is based on our clear understanding of how such sculpting takes place, as described below.

The Three As of Sculpting

Sculpting most commonly refers to forming, shaping and crafting figures and objects from a variety of materials, including ivory, marble, ice and clay. However, the term can also be applied to molding or shaping one's mindset or, more specifically, one's attitude and outlook at any age. Regardless of what is being shaped, in order to achieve success, the sculptor must possess the following traits:

- Attitude
- Adaptability
- Audacity

Attitude: Attitude is our mental state, forged by our beliefs and past experiences. Having a positive attitude is having a hopeful state of mind, which is achieved by anticipating a successful outcome in most, if not all, situations.

> Your attitude, not your aptitude, will determine your altitude.
> — Zig Ziglar, motivational speaker

Adaptability: Adaptability is our ability to freely and willingly respond to changing conditions. When things change, it is important to be willing and able to be flexible in order to adapt to the demands and challenges of the moment.

It is not the strongest species that survive,

nor the most intelligent,

but the ones most responsive to change.

— Charles Darwin

Audacity: Audacity is our willingness to take valiant steps; to be bold enough to take risks in our quest to achieve goals, even if they may seem impossible to attain. The sculptor is never satisfied with the outcome of his or her efforts, and instead keeps challenging and pushing himself or herself to achieve better outcomes.

Success is the child of audacity.

— Benjamin Disraeli,

Prime Minister of UK (1874-1880)

Each of these characteristics — attitude, adaptability and audacity — are essential and complementary components in the process of sculpting. Any one of them is not a substitute for the other; all three are needed to achieve the desired result.

Just as a sculptor chooses what to create, so must we choose how to live our final years. Quality of life at any age is a choice, and many seniors approach these choices as seen below:

Whiners: These are seniors who lack the positive attitude, adaptability and audacity needed for a good quality of life in their later years. They view old age as a wretched path to a dead end, often blaming fate for their misery.

Dreamers: Some seniors have a positive attitude about their retirement years, but they may have difficulty adapting to their changing circumstances, or they may not be assertive enough to pursue a better quality of life. These dreamers spend their later years wishfully thinking that, one day, they will somehow find a better life without putting in the effort to make it happen. As a result, that day never comes and their lives drag on in mediocrity and/or misery.

Dejected: These seniors are a frustrated bunch. In their pre-retirement years, they may have been quite successful, with positive attitudes, adaptability and audacity. However, in their post-retirement lives, they fall victim to the wrong beliefs about aging. Rather than viewing it as an adventurous and liberating phase, they develop a negative mindset of aging and see it as a dreadful end to their lives. Their negative attitudes often leave them confused and frustrated, causing them to lose interest in life itself.

Sculptors: Unlike the first three categories, this is a much smaller group of seniors who continue to maintain positive attitudes about their later years, despite the challenges of aging. Not only do they learn to look beyond their limitations, but they also use their attitude, adaptability and audacity identify and/or create opportunities for a better quality of life in their later years. Driven by their positive mindset, they challenge themselves to continue to pursue success by establishing audacious goals for themselves.

Raghu and I are sculptors. Driven by our pursuit of excellence and our commitment to providing service to others, we have positive mindsets that allow us to seek inspiration and pursue bold goals to sculpt better life for each of us, as well as others. In fact, we are currently studying other communities that are considered models for seniors seeking happier lifestyles and longer lives. These include:

- Athens Village in Athens, OH, where more than 100 seniors have formed a family, of sorts, to care for each other in their senior years.

- Roseto, PA, a tiny, close-knit community near the Lehigh Valley, where residents experienced a lower rate of heart disease and other life-threatening health issues and diseases than the rest of the nation.

- Five global Blue Zones, where people appear to live longer and happier lives than anywhere else on the planet. These include Sardinia, Italy; Okinawa, Japan; Ikaria, Greece; Nicoya, Costa Rica; and Loma Linda, CA.

Raghu and I realize this is a formidable goal; nevertheless, it is an extremely noble calling for us to try to make a positive difference in the lives of many people. Hopefully, we will prevail and this will become our legacy. We also hope our actions give credence to the following words of wisdom:

It is in your hands to create a better world for all who live in it.
— Nelson Mandala

Chapter 6

Meaningful Aging –

A Personal Responsibility

The victim mindset dilutes the human potential.
By not accepting personal responsibility for our circumstances,
we greatly reduce our power to change them.
— Steve Maraboli,
motivational speaker and best-selling author

Dolores Cummins

Strategic advisor, corporate educator and author

Queensland, Australia

Let us revisit my friend Jay in Chapter One who, in his late 70s, had given
up on life and asked me: "Is there a way for us to simply fold our hands,

say goodbye and be gone?" Unfortunately, three years after asking that question, Jay departed from this world amidst agony and confusion.

Why do many seniors like Jay find themselves in such an unfortunate situation? Because they are unprepared to navigate one of the biggest transitions of their lives – retirement. As a result, they become miserable and depend upon others to get them out of their whirlpool of misery. It is imperative that seniors learn to manage transitions, especially before and during their journey after retirement, and take personal responsibility for making their life worth living with meaning.

How can we learn to manage transitions and become responsible and resilient in the final chapters of our lives? We will search for that answer through the experiences of Dolores Cummins, a strategic adviser, corporate educator and co-author of *ALTITUDE—Two Women's Journey on Mount Kili-manjaro*. Ms. Cummins, who is approaching age 60, already has learned to take responsibility for the major transitions in her life. Here's her story.

Transitions

By Dolores Cummins

MEANINGFUL AGING

Each stage of our life carries thresholds to pass through to the next stage, chapter or path. Each threshold evokes a range of complex and at times confusing emotions, including fear, excitement, anticipation, anxiety and hope. Fear of the unknown, excitement about new possibilities, anticipation of new beginnings, anxiety about next steps and hope that the new chapter will fulfill us at a deep level and that we will be ok, we will be happy and we will stay safe.

It takes courage to step into the unknown. It also requires us to be responsible for our choices; a willingness to stay in the driver's seat, to chart our course and live our life in a way that brings meaning to us regardless of the judgements and dictates of others. Life calls us forward and we must answer its call with courage, with faith, with determination and with a commitment to living and not just existing. It also requires us to trust in ourselves – that we can determine our own life; in fact that we must. This is ultimately fulfilling.

I would like to share three major thresholds that not only helped me to forge a dynamic mindset of taking personal responsibility to prepare and navigate the unknown with faith, courage and commitment, but also made me aware of the challenges of the ultimate threshold when we are powerless to make choices and unable to take responsibility for ourselves.

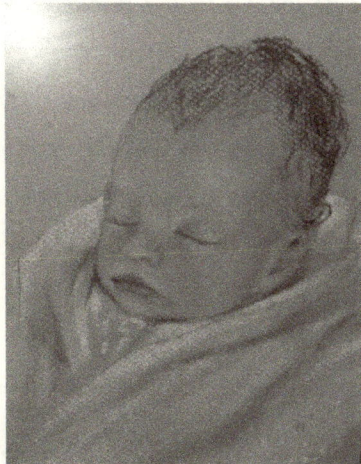

Alexander – My Sleeping Angel

The doctor turned to me and dropped the words that could never be taken back: "I'm afraid your baby has died."

Such simple words — such profound meaning. Who could fathom their depth, their lifelong implications? These fateful words remain etched indelibly in my soul.

Sitting in that sterile hospital room, my mind went numb. My eyes flew to the blue sky beyond the open window. Everything seemed to slow down. Time seemed to stop. I wondered absently why he would say such a thing. Whatever for? Perhaps he was trying to distract me from the escalating contractions. His words meant nothing. After all, my baby was alive and healthy, wasn't he? He was kicking strongly only a few short hours earlier. Everything was going as planned. Yet everything had stopped!

In the shocking silence, my mind screamed, "No. This is not happening. This is not real." Somewhere deep inside, however, the reality could not be denied. The doctor was saying something about the oxygen being cut off. The nurturing cord that had sustained my precious baby over the last nine months now brought his death. Shaking uncontrollably, the unbelievable news settled in. My mind desperately tried to make sense of this desolation.

The death of my first son Alexander awakened me to the beauty and fragility of life. I made a promise to Alexander that I would honor my life and his by living with courage, commitment and compassion. I would take personal responsibility for my life and I would challenge the boundaries of the possible, whether that was in climbing mountains, presenting to large audiences or raising my children to stand in their power and take responsibility for their lives.

After he passed, I completed my studies in psychotherapy, executive coaching, training and neurolinguistics. I started my own company, running training programs designed to awaken people to their life purpose. Later, I designed and presented leadership programs, as I believe we desperately need courageous, informed, self-aware and emotionally intelligent leaders.

Initially such personal change was a daunting and scary task, requiring courage and commitment. Clarity did not come easily as I had always considered myself a fairly shy, behind-the-scenes person. Indeed, the first time I spoke in front of a large audience, I was so nervous that I was shaking and my voice trembled as I took the stage. However, knowing that the new path was important, I had to learn how to walk it step by step.

My Husband – The Loving Protector

Dolores Cummins with her husband and children

My husband died when my twins Nicholas and Samantha were 14 years old. This was a tremendously challenging time in so many ways – emotionally, physically, mentally and spiritually. Much was called into question. As a mother, I couldn't replace the unquestioning innocence of children believing that all is well and safe in the world. Losing their dad at such an early age shattered any such illusion. I couldn't take their pain away, nor make it better. All I could do was be there for them, love them fiercely and walk part of their journey with them, trusting that they would come through this and emerge on the other side – changed certainly; stronger hopefully.

My children turn 21 this year and I am tremendously proud of who they have become. Wise beyond their years, they are both deeply empathic and thoughtful with a desire to make a difference. They will undoubtedly contribute to the world in their own unique way.

As the main provider for the family, I was also challenged to step up and keep the show on the road – to manage the financial demands of daily life, school fees, mortgage, etc. I had to push through personal barriers, self-doubts and anxious moments to build a strong business that would support us financially while giving me the flexibility to be present at school events, sports days, parent-teacher meetings and graduations.

Living in Australia, thousands of miles from my family in Ireland, meant that I had to take responsibility and be accountable for every aspect of parenting and working. I was often reminded of the phrase "If it's to be, it's up to me." Life demands personal responsibility at every stage.

Turning 60 has prompted me to reevaluate what matters, including where to focus my energy and time. Time appears more finite now and therefore more precious. Time is not to be squandered, as there is less of it ahead than behind, and I realized I also must take time to prepare myself to live my life meaningfully in my golden years whenever it occurs.

While taking care of my dear father who passed away in 2015, and currently taking care of my mom in elderly care, I got a glimpse of the final frontier of the human journey, where the ability to make choices and take responsibility not only becomes difficult, but is also impossible. I would like to share my mom's story of transition and what happened when she no longer has ability to make her own choices.

MY LOVING MOM – THE FINAL FRONTIER

Dolores Cummins (left) connecting with her mother

The Elsewhere Place

It's 4.30 in the morning and my return flight from Dublin to Brisbane is in a few short hours. Not time yet to emerge from my cozy bed on this frosty morning. Temperatures hover around -1c (31F). The persistent sounds from below prevent me from returning to sleep. What is that noise, I wonder sleepily? The TV? Music? A computer game? My drowsy brain tries to make sense of it, this loud noise. I wonder: does the person responsible not realize the time?

Descending the stairs, it's cold. Are there lights on in the kitchen? As I reach the bottom, I see there before me, fumbling with the front door, my lovely mom. She turns quickly, startled – like a wild animal in the headlights. She looks uncomprehendingly at me. "It's okay mom. It's only me. What's wrong?" I ask. "I'm scared," she says, in a small frightened voice.

Fighting back the tears, I gently take her hand, looking deeply into her eyes to enable me to connect across the confusion and fear. "It's okay mom.

You're safe. You're at Jacqui's house. Nothing to be frightened of here." I lead her back to her bedroom. She's agitated and wide awake. "It's okay mom," I repeat softly. She grips my hand tightly, holding onto this tenuous connection.

She had a bad dream — a dream where she found herself in a place where no one knew her and she was totally lost. She says to me in that same small voice "I used to be somebody. ..." Sadness, bewilderment and anxiety all sit under those few words.

Over the past three weeks, she often seems confused and has difficulty engaging in conversation or responding to questions. This is not the strong-willed, fiercely independent mom I know. Sometimes, she seems like a vacant shell as she sits staring into space. Where are you mom, I wonder?

I ask her how she feels. She doesn't know. I ask her what she's scared of. She doesn't know. I ask her what she needs or what she wants. She doesn't know.

My heart aches for her absence. Over the past few weeks, we've had time together. Sometimes she's here. Sometimes, she's far, far away, some-where else. What happens in that elsewhere place; a place I can't enter, but seek to understand?

My mom is disappearing, just like my dad did before he died, and I feel helpless.

My mom never wanted to go into an aged-care home. She wanted to stay in her own home, doing her own thing, in control of her destiny and daily routine. Not much to ask really. This is the home she grew up in. It's the home where we were all born — seven children in total. It's the home she shared with my dad for nearly 60 years. Her home. Her sanctuary. Her memory palace. But how can she stay here now? She can hardly walk, let alone climb the stairs to her bedroom on the first floor. She uses a set of wheels to get around — "the best thing ever invented," she told me one day.

She no longer knows how to care for herself. She no longer knows how to answer her phone or use the kettle. Such simple things have become complex and incomprehensible tasks. It's like watching a beautiful stained-glass window fall apart, piece by piece.

She knows something is wrong and struggles to find the words to express that "wrongness." In an earlier, more lucid moment, she explained that she felt like part of her was elsewhere, that part of her was missing. She struggled to express the frustration, anxiety and fear of waking up to a foreign world each day, where nothing was familiar and where she had to piece together bits of information to help work out where or who she was. She struggles to orient herself to an increasingly confusing world of strangers and strangeness.

Where's my mom? I see only glimpses now of the once strong and feisty woman. Is she still here behind the confused eyes that glaze over when the conversation becomes too much effort to follow or find the right words to communicate? Who is she becoming? Where does she disappear when she is absent?

I want to gather her up and find a magic pill to make it all better, to stop the night descending; to bring security into the spiraling confusion, support in the darkness and a pathway out of the elsewhere place. But I don't know how. She is descending into the twilight zone where the boundary between reality shifts and the question of what's real emerges and dissolves.

Her daily struggle is apparent. Sometimes she seems to be desperately holding onto a fragmented reality. While I can't change it, what I can do is put structures in place to keep her safe and secure; to remind her of who she is and reassure her of how precious and loved she is.

Today my mom is peaceful. She has adjusted to her new home and has accepted her changed circumstances.

Joseph Campbell said: "The privilege of a lifetime is being who you are."

Navigating transitions require awareness and skills. At each fork in the road, there is a time to make decisions, a time to celebrate, a time to grieve, a time to let go and a time to move forward, sometimes hesitantly. Sometimes we need support with our first tentative steps.

How we manage ambiguity and uncertainty is a major factor in determining how responsible we will be in the transitions of our life. Some steps to help include the following;

1. **Build awareness.** When faced with transition, it is vital to acknowledge that change is a process which, once understood, enables you to make sense of the journey. This awareness is the first step.

2. **Acknowledge endings.** Let go! This is a time of letting go, of releasing past relationships, careers, possessions, ways of being, lifestyles and perhaps more. In letting go, we commit to moving on. This may also be a time of coming to terms with changed circumstances. Sometimes, in order to let go, we need to forgive somebody who hurt us or did us wrong. The act of forgiveness is powerful.

3. **The bridge between realities – sitting with the unknown.** Now you must negotiate the neutral zone – the bridge to new beginnings. This can be a confusing, in-between time when we are not sure what to do next. It is a time of reflection, questioning, regrouping and reevaluating our situation and/or sense of purpose. This phase requires courage, honesty and commitment to a new journey.

   Our ability to cope with ambiguity and uncertainty is challenged. It is normal at this point to yearn for the apparent safety of the past, which beckons alluringly; however, to retreat there has a high cost.

Why risk all for an illusion of safety? It is time to drop old familiar patterns, habits and behaviors so you can define your new rules.

The only real security in this world is within you. It stems from knowing at a deep visceral level that no matter what life throws at you, no matter what lies around the corner, you will cope and come through – perhaps a little battered, perhaps a little less egocentric, definitely a little wiser and ultimately unbowed and ready to continue the journey we call life.

4. **Explore new beginnings.** The final stage in transition requires an exploration of new beginnings. It demands curiosity, flexibility and openness. Trust and a willingness to explore new possibilities are essential; commitment and courage will see you through.

Become aware of your values and your motivations. Learn new behaviors and new skills. Forge new patterns that eventually become new beliefs and new habits.

This can be quite a challenge, yet without a commitment to navigating new paths, we risk living a diminished life; an existence devoid of deeper meaning. The words of Soren Kierkegaard, a Danish philosopher, resonate with me: "To dare is to lose one's footing momentarily. To not dare is to lose oneself."

In a poignant but mystical way, my little Alexander, my beloved husband, and my dear mom have awakened me to the realities of human life and have inspired me to take responsibility to manage transitions by navigating new paths to fulfillment. Questions for each of us to take responsibility of our circumstances and to navigate new paths may include: Who are you? What is your identity? What do you stand for? What are your driving values and internal motivators? Where are you going? How do you want to

75

define your future? When you can answer these questions, you can step fully into life understanding that it's not what happens to us but rather how we respond that defines us.

Navigating Transitions

If it's to be, it's up to me. Life calls us forward and we must answer its call to pass through thresholds to the next stage. It requires managing transitional emotions, making choices and navigating new paths while taking responsibility of our choices and actions.

The above essence of Dolores Cummins' life experiences says it all about developing and deploying a dynamic mindset of taking responsibility to face and navigate various transitions of our life. By sharing her heart-wrenching personal tragedies of losing her first child and her husband and witnessing her mother's struggle to accept and adjust in her new circumstances, Ms. Cummins has eloquently demonstrated that a dynamic mindset of personal responsibility helps us to not only cross the transitional thresholds, but also provides us opportunities to charter new and uplifting paths.

Taking personal responsibility for the changed circumstances of our lives —like starting the journey after retirement — requires skills to manage the changes in a proactive and genial way. The four skills outlined by Ms. Cummins — *building awareness, acknowledging endings, bridging realities and exploring new beginnings* — are remarkable assets, not only in our advanced years, but also in every phase of the aging process.

Although Dolores Cummins is years away from starting her journey into the golden years, she has already equipped herself with a dynamic mindset built on personal responsibility for managing transitional challenges. Unlike many seniors, who start their golden years with expectations of freedom and entitlement and quickly feel disappointed and discouraged by the realities they face, those following Ms. Cummins' four-step process of awareness, acknowledging ending, bridging and exploring will definitely start their golden years with a realistic understanding of what lies ahead and a plan for how to make it meaningful.

> ***The moment you take responsibility for everything in your life is the moment you can change anything in life.***
> – Hal Elrod, motivational speaker
> and author of the bestselling book
> *The Miracle Morning.*

Chapter 7
Continual Learning
for Meaningful Aging

Live as if you were to die tomorrow.
Learn as if you were to live forever.
— Mahatma Gandhi

Vishwakant G. Mankodi

Tavares, Florida

Several people rushed to congratulate Vishwakant Mankodi as he finished performing classic melodies with the harmonium, a reed organ mostly used in Indian music, at the Shantiniketan Retirement Community in Florida. The songs were not only nostalgic for the assembled seniors, but both the music and his singing were quite soothing.

Enchanted by his performance, I caught up with the 87year-old Mr. Mankodi afterwards to learn more about him and his incredible talent. "You must have practiced for a long time to learn to play the harmonium and sing along with it so well," I said.

"No," he answered. "Singing and playing the harmonium have been my hobbies for a long time. Although I occasionally sang in public over the past 35 years, and I have performed on the harmonium in public as well, I didn't feel comfortable singing and playing at the same time. That required practice, which I didn't have time for while I was working, due to my hectic schedule.

"After my retirement, with more free time at my disposal, I thought it might be a good time to learn how to sing along with the harmonium, but I brushed off the idea, thinking I was by then too old to learn. I also convinced myself that the increasing arthritis in my knees would soon spread to my other joints, including my hands, so I probably wouldn't be able to play the harmonium much longer, anyway. Despite these excuses, I knew in my heart that I still wanted to learn to sing and play someday, so the thought was always in the back of my mind."

"Then, how did you get to where you are now, able to sing and play so masterfully?" I asked.

"My past caught up with me and I had no choice," he replied, with an odd smile.

Completely puzzled, I begged him to elaborate. He explained:

Retirement is a strange phase of life. It takes you to your past and makes you reflect on your triumphs and tribulations. That reflection made me aware of the fact that life has offered me great opportunities, which often required me to learn new things in a hurry. I realized how much I thrived because of those opportunities. Quick learning and achieving excellence have been embedded in my mindset since my college days in my native state of Gujarat, India, when I took up sports and won several college, inter-college, and university championships in Table Tennis, Badminton, and Tennis. I also won state championship in Table Tennis.

My work life followed the same pattern of learning things quickly to achieve excellence. After receiving two undergraduate degrees in mechanical and electrical engineering, I taught mechanical engineering to college students for two years and then transitioned into an unfamiliar job — selling parts for equipment used in the textile and rubber industries. The father of a close friend of mine recommended me to T. Smith PVT, LTD. which functioned as manufacturers' representatives in India for several American and European companies such as Uniroyal Inc. of USA, Ateliers Roannais De Constructions Textiles of France, Rubber Regeneration Company of Manchester, England, and a few other European companies.

On joining T. Smith company, I was sent for six months to England, France, Switzerland, Germany and other western European countries to meet the management of the companies' marketing components through our agency. On return, with hard work, I quickly learned the customer base, as well as what they required in terms of quality for the parts, in addition to import regulations for foreign commodities being brought into India and tax obligations established by the central and state governments. In a span of six years, from 1961 to 1967, I was promoted from Senior Technical Sales Representative to Director of Sales. I thrived in that business, and I became a minority shareholder in the company.

For the next four years, from 1967 to 1971, I joined EMVI Enterprises as Chief Executive/Managing Partner. EMVI was engaged in promoting the products of American, British and Japanese companies like Uniroyal of USA, Sumitoms Naugatuck Company of Japan and Lastex Yarn and Lactron Thread of London. In 1971, I joined Aprocot Agencies as Chief Executive/Managing Director to organize the marketing of special cots and aprons to cotton textile mills in India. I managed that company for seven years, until 1978. As the future of the textile industry was getting bleak with more and more companies closing and being taken over by the National Textile Corporation of India (NTC), I decided to move on to new opportunities.

I knew that some of my college friends had emigrated to the United States and were doing quite well. I had visited a few of them in 1975, and was very much impressed by the American way of life and the ease of doing business there. My friends had tried to coax me into moving to the United States, but at the time, I was a successful businessman enjoying life in India. However, with the declining situation of the textile industry, I made up my mind to emigrate to the United States in 1977.

I was 44 years old at the time. Starting our new life in the United States, I joined a subsidiary of the Sippican consulting firm, which was helping the United States Army to develop a brand-new military city KKMC (King Khalid Military City) in Al-Batin, Saudi Arabia. I spent nine years in that company as a design engineer, during which I had to learn many new things quickly, including the Fortran computer programming language, which was essential for scientific calculations and programming design codes. I didn't at-

tend any school to become proficient in this computer language, but instead taught myself and became quite skillful in using it.

In 1987, a friend of mine made me aware of another new opportunity — marketing oriental rugs imported from India and South Asian countries. Seeing that as more lucrative and more interesting than my job at that time, I jumped into that unfamiliar yet intriguing field. With the active support and encouragement from my wife Sandhya, who worked as a project leader for Parker Brothers from 1981 to 1992 in their IT department and for Rockport Shoes from 1992 to 2001 in IT database administration, I learned the market dynamics and import regulations for the rug business and developed a very successful business of selling rugs in the New England area for more than 15 years. During that period, we raised and educated two great kids, a daughter and a son, both of whom are now productive members of the American society. Our daughter, a physician, is currently the medical director of the Northshore Physicians Group, and our son, who majored as a communication engineer, is the managing director of a large private equity firm.

Though his background and credentials were impressive, Mr. Mankodi still hadn't answered my question about learning to sing while playing the harmonium. I was about to interrupt his story when he tied it all together:

Reflecting on my past achievements, including learning new and difficult things, made me aware that the primary reason for the successes in my life was my unflinching dedication and disciplined effort to learn — and that was missing from my quest to learn to sing while playing the harmonium.

I realized that I had half-heartedly tried to learn before, but had given up too soon. On top of that, I was using my old age as a convenient excuse for not trying again. In addition, I realized that my fear of arthritis in my knees spreading to other parts of my body, including my hands, was overblown. Sure, the arthritis in my knees limited my ability to play tennis. However, it didn't affect my fingers or my voice. So, I realized it was time to focus on achieving my goal — this time with the zeal for learning that had helped me achieve success in the past. So one day, after playing the harmonium for another singer, I shut the case and declared to myself: I will only open this harmonium in public when I can also sing with it."

"How did you feel after making that commitment to yourself?" I inquired.

Smiling, Mr. Mankodi replied: "Relieved — and confident that I would not fail this time. And that is exactly what happened. In less than three years, with disciplined practice and continual inspiration from Purshottam Upadhyay, a musical legend and a close friend who was awarded the Padmashri Medal in 2017 — the fourth highest civilian award in the republic of India — I was able to master the intricacies of synchronizing my singing with the music of my harmonium."

"You must have been elated when you sang while playing the harmonium for the first time in public," I said.

"Yes! Whereas I had been confident that I would meet this challenge, seeing the pleasant look of surprise on the faces of my close friends, and especially my wife, when they saw me singing with my harmonium for the first time was priceless," he said.

Mr. Mankodi may seem like an exception to the rule when it comes to trying and learning new things or perfecting skills in an existing passion during our advanced years. Many seniors tend to believe prevailing myths such as *you can't teach old dog new tricks;* or *learning is for the young;* or *there is nothing left to learn in old age.* In reality, Mr. Mankodi is not an exception, but rather an example of how a growing number of seniors are deciding to pursue their passions and/or learn new things in their later years.

Contrary to conventional wisdom that learning is difficult or impossible later in life, our brains exhibit astounding potency in our advanced years if we choose to keep challenging ourselves. David Robson, author of the book *The Intelligence Trap: Why Smart People Make Stupid Mistakes* and a former editor, BBC *Future,* an online news site, provides evidence of the brain's potential in later years in his article on BBC *Future:* The Amazing Fertility of the Older Mind:

> *If you ever fear that you are already too old to learn a new skill, remember **Priscilla Sitienei**, a midwife from Ndalat in rural Kenya. Having grown up without primary school education, she had never learned to read or write. As she approached her twilight years, she wanted to note down her experiences and knowledge to pass down to the next generation. And so, she started to attend lessons at the local school – along with six of her great-great-grandchildren. She was 90 at the time.*
>
> *Just consider the case of **Aleksandar Hemon**. Originally from Sarajevo in then-Yugoslavia, he found himself stranded in the United States at the outbreak of the Bosnian war in 1992 – despite having little command of English. "I had this horrible, pressing need to write because things were happening. I needed to do it the same way I needed to eat, but I just had no language to write in," he later told the* New York Times. *And so he set about embracing the language on the streets around him. Within three years, he had published his first piece in an*

American journal, a path that eventually led to three critically ac-claimed novels, two short story collections, a book of autobiographical essays and a MacArthur Genius Award.

How can we join the ranks of Vishwakant Mankodi, Priscilla Sitienei, Aleksandar Hemon and others in continually learning new things or perfect-ing skills in existing passions in our advanced years, creating happiness in the process? The answer is not to pray for instant learning, but rather to unlock the treasure of continuous learning by using a combination of the following three elements:

- Humility
- Commitment
- Sharing

Humility: Irrespective of age, humility is a prerequisite for learning. In our senior years, with all of our wisdom and experience, we may wrongly start to believe that we already know it all, so there is no need to learn anything else. Quite frankly, this belief must be quashed. To quote Mahat-ma Gandhi: "It is unwise to be too sure of one's own wisdom."

Mr. Mankodi demonstrated humility by acknowledging his inability to simultaneously sing and play the harmonium, and taking it upon himself to learn how to synchronize the two.

It is important to avoid the trap of being overconfident as to the extent of your knowledge and instead acknowledge with humility when you need to learn new things or perfect a skill.

Commitment: The second key to learning is a commitment. How many times do we decide to learn new things or accomplish tasks, only to put them off? Many of us fail to follow through and instead find excuses to jus-tify our failure to do so.

President Abraham Lincoln once said: "Commitment is what transforms a promise into reality." But without understanding its true definition, commitment is just a hollow word.

A commitment is a pledge to yourself or others to carry through on your stated intentions. The process of transforming intentions into results requires desire, determination and discipline. All three are indispensable. *Desire* is our yearning or hoping for an outcome. *Determination* reflects the firm resolve to succeed in achieving that outcome. *Discipline* is required for mastery of the skills required to achieve that goal.

In addition to embracing humility, Mr. Mankodi kept his commitment to himself by keeping lit the flame of his desire to sing while playing the harmonium; by displaying an unflinching determination to succeed in learning how to synchronize his singing with the music; and by his disciplined efforts to practice until he was able to master the skills necessary to do so.

Sharing: Sharing what one has learned bolsters the learning process and retention of this knowledge as shown below, through a series of steps, with each step building upon the previous one:

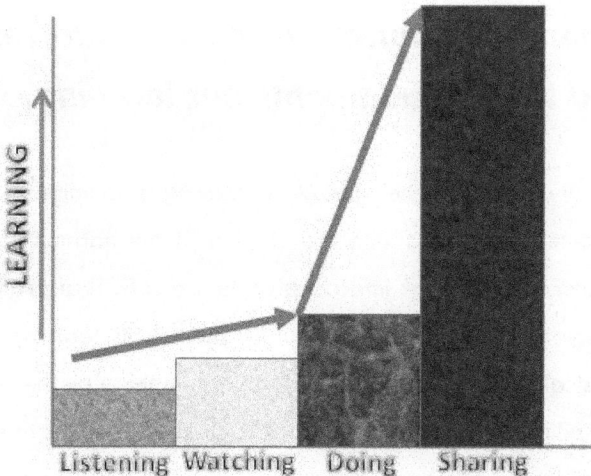

Baldev K Seekri

87

If we want to learn a new task or activity, the process often begins by listening to someone else explaining how to do it. We gain additional understanding by watching someone perform the task or activity, and our learning is further enhanced when we actually do it ourselves. By sharing this information with others, we reinforce our retention of the knowledge, which causes our learning to increase exponentially.

The learning process doesn't end with sharing. In fact, it begins the learning process anew. As a teacher shares information and instructions with others, the teacher often discovers intricacies about the subject matter, leading to additional knowledge of the material and a quest for more information. So the teacher, in effect, becomes a student while acquiring additional information by listening, watching and doing, and then shares this additional knowledge by teaching it to his or her students. These teacher-student-teacher transformations continue endlessly.

For me, learning and sharing what I have learned have become my primary passion and brought joy to my existence during my senior years.

Humility is the prerequisite for learning; commitment transmutes our desires into results; and sharing augments our learning.

Mr. Mankodi did exactly the same. After making a commitment to learn how to synchronize his singing with the playing of the harmonium, he repeatedly practiced to learn the intricacies of the process. That practice was not done in isolation; he instead continually shared his learning with his friend and musical legend Purshottam Upadhyay. In this way, he continued to improve his skills until he felt confident enough in his abilities to share his singing with harmonium with the public.

Forging a Dynamic Mindset
of Continual Learning in Old Age

While humility, commitment and sharing are indispensable elements for any type of learning if we are to keep our mindset dynamic, it is also vital for seniors to keep their minds sharp and robust. The prime impediments on this front are often a fear of memory loss and negligence when it comes to keeping our brains healthy.

Fear of Memory Loss: As we age, one of the biggest fears many of us have is memory loss. This fear may cause us to avoid routine activities and shirk away from learning new things. Many of us start relying on various tools for assistance or support. For example, many seniors rely on GPS devices for driving directions, even if they have travelled a particular route many times. Some of us have even kept traditional maps in our vehicles, along with the GPS, in case the device malfunctions.

No doubt, with age, cognitive decline sets in and, for sure, our memories aren't as sharp as they were when we were young. However, this fear of memory loss tends to be overblown and can actually serve as a self-fulfilling prophecy that appears to contribute to the premature decline of our memory. This, in turn, can result in the loss of our confidence to keep learning.

Lack of confidence to learn new things can be driven by our mental attitude towards memory. "I'm too old to learn anything new; I won't remember it anyway." That's a frequent justification for our refusal to try to learn new skills, or our apparent inability to retain them for future use. However, an increasing number of psychologists now say that a person's mental attitude towards memory loss and aging could play a bigger role than most people might think. Studies show that a positive attitude leads to some people reporting that they feel younger than their years, with less reluctance when it comes to trying new things. This youthful outlook often results in them being more active and more inclined to rely on their memory instead of using memory aids. In other words, some of our perceptions about limitations as we age may be self-fulfilling prophecies, rather than actual physical or mental effects of the aging process.

Staying confident by exuding a positive attitude and rejecting the presumption of limitations that comes with aging can go a long way towards succeeding, especially when it comes to adopting a mindset of continual learning. You can see that confidence and positive attitude in these words of Martina Navratilova, a tennis legend who continued to learn and excel at the game even in her later years: "The tennis ball doesn't know how old I am."

Neglecting the health of our brain: What good is our extended life without a healthy brain? Many seniors don't pay as much attention to maintaining and/or improving the health of their brains as they do their bodies. This results from a common belief that, as we get older, our brains will deteriorate faster, leading to memory loss. But this isn't necessarily always the case. Yes, our brains may be less efficient than when we were younger, but they will continue to serve us quite well. Ongoing research – and the documented accomplishments of many seniors achieving unprecedented successes in various endeavors – are testimony to the fact that most of us are able to learn new things and create new memories throughout the aging process.

Contrary to the conventional belief that the aging brain is a perpetual liability, it might be more thoughtful than originally believed. According to Judith Horstman, author of *The Scientific American: Day in the Life of Your Brain*, points out that as we age, our brain also has amassed a lifetime of experiences and accumulated wisdom that can lead to better decision-making.

To keep our brains healthy and nimble, in addition to physical activity, we must challenge ourselves by tackling new and difficult tasks, such as learning a new language or solving a puzzle; increasing socialization to minimize loneliness and improve our immune system and memory; engaging in religious and spiritual activity to reduce stress; and eating wisely to reduce obesity.

These days, when I watch Mr. Mankodi singing while playing his harmonium, I see a man who is becoming a little frail, but he also exudes a greater sense of happiness and contentment. He is living and not just existing; he's not simply waiting for the dreaded end of his life. By sharing the story of how he learned new skills to pursue his passion in his later years, he has given hope to all of us seniors. His story proves that getting older can be productive and joyful if we constantly learn new things or perfect skills needed to pursue our passions. The more we do to keep our minds sharp and robust, the easier it will be for us to continue to learn, keeping us productive and joyful as we live through the last phase of our lives.

Once you stop learning, you start dying.
– Albert Einstein

Chapter 8

Purposeful Passions

for Meaningful Aging

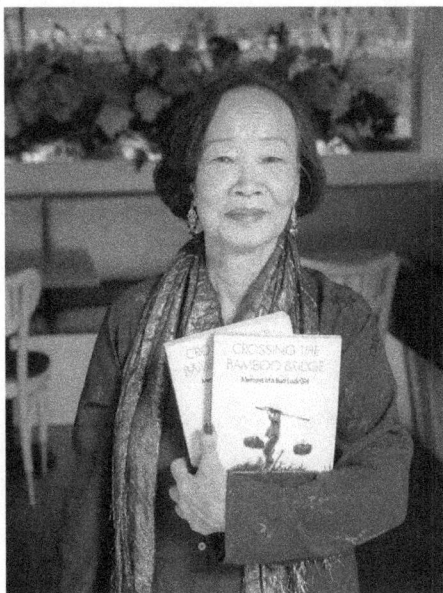

Mai Donohue

Author, Chef, Educator, Motivational Speaker, Mentor

"You will be a good teacher someday," my teacher Mr. Ban told me when I was 12 years old. On my way home from school that day, my feet barely touched the ground. I was singing and skipping without a worry in the world. I thought of how happy my mother would be to hear what my teacher had said. Instead, my mother met me at the door to our home and immediately ordered me to do chores including feeding the pigs, making dinner and hauling in water to fill the barrel.

"But mother, I want to tell you what my teacher said..."

She didn't even let me finish the sentence before she walked out the door.

The next morning, with my hands folded, I asked her permission to go to school. She didn't answer. Instead, she told me: "Mai, you can't go to school anymore." She explained that my brother Ming would be attending school from now on, instead of me. He was young, but he was a boy. My mother believed he needed to go to school so he could take care of her in her old age. I, on the other hand, was just a girl and my mother had other plans for me. She announced that I would be getting married to a man named Binh, whom I had never even met.

I blurted out: "Mother, do what you want with me, but, for the thousandth time, I don't want to marry."

Within the year, I was married. Soon after, I was pregnant and gave birth to my first son Han when I was 15 years old.

The year was 1965. The Vietnam War was at its peak. This teenage bride had begun a life of sheer misery with a brutal husband who regularly beat her and once left her on the side of the road, thinking she was dead. She seemed destined to a lifetime of suffering, like so many other impoverished and oppressed young girls in her war-ravaged country of Vietnam. Instead, she fled, leaving everything and everyone behind, risking her life to escape from the nightmare of poverty and abuse.

Fast forward to 2019. That unfortunate young girl is Mai Donohue, who is now a retired teacher's aide, author and motivational speaker whose pursuit of her childhood dream to help teach others led her from a life of destitution in Vietnam to a successful career and family life in America. She has seven children and 14 grandchildren and lives in the historic community of Barrington, RI, with her husband, Brian Donohue, a retired Naval officer.

MEANINGFUL AGING

The story of her remarkable journey through life was featured in a 2006 PBS documentary called *Mai: A Lesson in Courage, Passion and Hope*, which was nominated for a New England Emmy Award.

It also was the subject of her autobiography, which she wrote and published in 2016. Her book, *Crossing the Bamboo Bridge — Memoirs of a Bad Luck Girl,* is a captivating autobiography that tells the story of how she beat all odds to realize the American dream. The book is receiving very high praise from readers.

On the recommendation of a friend, I read her book and felt inspired with her courage to face a multitude of adversities throughout her life imposed by relatives and strangers alike.

What forces allowed Mai Donohue to persevere in the face of never ending string of adversities — an abusive mother, a brutal husband, a ritual-bound brother, many wolves dressed as relatives and well-wishers, and numerous challenges involved in moving and adjusting to a new country far away?

What transformed Mrs. Donahue's life was not only the great love provided to her by her second husband, children and grandchildren, but also the power of her passion for learning and her determination to get an education for the larger purpose of helping others get their education, too. She went on to become a teacher's aide in an alternative education program at a high school in Barrington, RI, where she worked with students with behavioral issues for 15 years until her retirement in 2015.

The power of her passion for learning and pursuing her education was strikingly evident throughout her life. Barred from attending school by her mother, she took her brother's books to teach herself. She had no pencils and paper, so used her fingers to write notes in the dust. While working as household help for a cook in Saigon, she saved and hid the newspaper wrappings of raw fish to read them later. She also–tried to read magazines when she could find spare time during babysitting chores. She nearly starved herself to save money so she could attend classes to learn English during the ongoing war in Saigon.

She later met her husband Brian and came to America with him in 1970 and pursued her education here. She worked hard to earn a GED, then took classes at a community college for seven years to earn an associate degree in General Studies. She continued her studies at the University of Rhode Island, where she earned her bachelor of arts degree cum laude in 2002. Having reached her goal of completing her education and became an educator, she went on to fulfill her childhood teacher's prediction that she would be a good teacher and also, aligned her passion for learning with a larger purpose – helping students with behavioral issues in school.

Greatly intrigued by the amazing accomplishments Mai Donahue achieved in the face of tremendous adversity, I was curious as to how her passion for and pursuit of learning was helping Mrs. Donohue with the most recent challenge in her life – retirement. I wrote to Mai Donohue, asking her if she would share the story of her life in retirement for my book.

I am sincerely grateful for her willingness to share her story to help other seniors. Here, in her own words, is Mai Donohue's approach to retirement:

Bumping into Old Age

By Mai Donohue

Being old is not what I want.

If we are lucky, we live to our old age. Some even say it is a golden age. Not everyone agrees.

MEANINGFUL AGING

Growing old seems so unfair sometimes. The other day, I sat in a chair in the doctor's office and listened as my husband Brian, who has Parkinson's disease, told his doctor that lately he was moving more slowly, even unsteadily, on his feet. His doctor told him that if he wanted to improve his balance, he should start doing yoga or Tai Chi. Each time she suggested something to him, he said no. He said he was going to the gym every day and didn't need to do anything else. Finally, in a calm voice, she told him: "I know you work out daily and that is what is keeping you in shape. It's great. But you aren't just dealing with Parkinson's. You are also dealing with old age. There are no magic pills that will help you keep your balance. You have to work at it."

Getting old wasn't something that we thought about every day. We were busy raising our seven children. We were very happy to finally have our house to ourselves when they moved out, but we don't really have it to ourselves. Our children, like lucky pennies, keep coming back. And our family keeps growing. With spouses and grandchildren, we have quadrupled in size.

Thirteen years ago, in 2006 Brian was diagnosed with prostate cancer. In 2013, he was diagnosed with Parkinson's disease. In between, there have been other surgeries as well. It has all been very difficult. I have tried my best to be positive. I put on a happy face and went about my daily routine, taking care of my husband as best I could. In 2015, though, I had what the doctors called a mini-stroke, I could no longer pretend everything was okay. I was scared for both of us. I couldn't sleep. I cried and cried for no reason. Our children tried their best to make me happy, but it didn't work. Finally, my doctor suggested that I go see a psychologist.

The psychologist asked me what he could do to help. I told him that I was fine; that it was my doctor's idea to schedule this visit. I said therapy is for rich white men — not for me, a poor girl from the Vietnamese countryside, with no time or money for such a thing. My entire life, I have always taken care of my own problems. He looked at me and shook his head and said, "I understand that you don't think you need to see me, but mental illness is like any other illness. If you don't get to the root of the problem, it will spread."

I realized that I could save time and money by not going to therapy — or I could save myself. I was sick and tired of being sick and tired, so I chose to save myself. I went back to the psychologist for three more sessions and that helped me get back on track. It's like what the doctor had told my husband: there is no magic pill to make everything better. In life, it takes work to find your balance.

When I returned to work after my stroke, everyone was so happy to see me. I was a teacher's aide in the alternative learning program at Barrington High School, working with students who had behavioral issues. My students and my co-workers gave me so much love and support, but still something felt wrong with my life. My mind was so full of thoughts of getting old and wondering what good I was doing. I started to feel that I will not be 100 percent to do my job and started to think maybe it was time for me to move on. I retired in 2015.

I used to hear people say that they couldn't wait until they retired, but I never felt that way. I loved my job and the connection I had with the students, helping them get their education. Besides, retirement was for old people, not for me.

After retirement, I felt useless and disconnected from society. I was angry. I was losing my mind.

"Why me?" I asked. I had worked so hard all my life and for what? The years were passing and where was I going? I woke up early every day and went to the gym and went to work and ate healthy and went to church every Sunday. What more did God want from me?

I asked for help and got my answer: throughout my life, I had a habit of examining any problem that cursed my life, big or small. If there was something I didn't like, I found a way to change it. So, I decided to start a new chapter in my life.

I told myself I had two choices: I could be angry about my situation and unhappy for the rest of my life, or I could choose to be grateful to be alive.

I realized I shouldn't let my age affect my emotional well being. There was more to life than being old.

To be alive and to be old is not a punishment. I had complained that I wanted a better life, but I realized that to still be alive with my husband by my side every night is a gift. I promised myself that I would live every day like it is my last day of life.

Old age doesn't care about your gender or race, or if you are rich or poor. We all get older. And when it is time to go, I will go, but not without kicking and screaming to hold on to the life that I have. I will fight for this gift of life with my very last breath.

I started to focus on the things that brought me the most joy, such as the food I often share with people. I love to cook. It is my passion. Food, to me, isn't just something that fills your stomach; it also fills your heart. Food is love that I want to share. Food is like a gene — we carry it in our blood and pass it down from one generation to the next. It connects us, from one culture to another. It is an international language that we use. It is also a great joy in my life that helps me deal with old age.

I learned to cook when I was five years old. I wasn't very good at it, but hunger drove me to learn how to provide for myself and for my younger cousins, who were starving and needed to be fed. I caught field mice and made them into stew. I loved to see the smiles on the grateful faces of my cousins. When the war came to Vietnam, I escaped to Saigon and worked for rich people who hired the best cooks from around the country. These cooks took me under their wings. They taught me how to make all kinds of cuisine from all over the world: North Vietnamese, South Vietnamese, French, Indian, Chinese. By the time I met my current husband, then a handsome young US Naval officer, I could cook anything. I cooked my way into his heart.

Mai Donohue's Vietnamese Cooking

In 1970, we moved to the United States. At first, I left my Vietnamese cooking behind. I thought that my country's food was for the poor. Even though I was so homesick for Vietnamese food, I was afraid of what people would think of me and so I forced myself to eat hot dogs and hamburgers and learned how to make pizza from my American friends.

Eventually, I started making my Vietnamese food again — first for my family and then for friends and later for strangers.

I held fundraisers for Vietnamese orphanages and schools. After Hurricane Sandy, with the help of students and teachers at my school, I raised more than $22,000 to help rebuild a high school on Staten Island that had been destroyed by the storm.

Mai Donohue is rocking a full house at Books on the Square in Providence, RI, October 2017

Recently, my husband and I celebrated our 50th anniversary with more than 200 guests. I fed them Vietnamese food and raised more than $1,000 for Sophia Academy, a private middle school for underprivileged girls in Providence, RI.

Also, I decided to let go of my obsession about old age. I retired from my job in 2015 and started writing. The best thing about starting to write when you're older is that you have more stories to tell. In 2016, with the help and support of my family and my friends, I published my memoir, Crossing the Bamboo Bridge: Memoirs of a Bad Luck Girl. My book was a finalist for the best book by the Independent Publishers of New England. The Girl Scouts of Southeastern New England honored me as one of the 2018 Leading Woman of Distinction Award for my work as an author, educator and motivational speaker.

I continue to mentor students at Barrington High School with their senior projects. I invite friends to lunch and dinners and cook for them. This year, my husband and I published a book of his poetry, The Night Watch Poems, that he has been working on since before we met. I also continue to support my three favorite charities, the Girl Scouts of Southeastern New England, the Sophia Academy and the Southeast Asian Community.

Looking back on my life, I have no regrets. Despite the fact that my husband has Parkinson's disease and my stroke often makes my right hand and leg tingle, I am grateful to be alive. To be old isn't a bad thing. We are so lucky to be alive and to live in this country where there is new technology, new research and new medicines being created every day. We have the chance to live longer and I am grateful for it.

We have many friends that we met 40 or 50 years ago, when they were young, like us. Now some of them walk with walkers;

some still on their own. When we see each other, we are so happy to share our stories with each other. We compare who has the most grandchildren and Brian and I always win. Seven children and their spouses. Fourteen grandchildren. Thirty of us in total.

No matter how old I am, life is very good to this old Vietnamese girl."

Making Aging Our Ally

By sharing her life story, Mai Donohue has shown us the secret of making aging an ally in every stage of our life — pursuing our passions with unflinching dedication and aligning them to a larger purpose of serving others.

It was the power of her passion for pursuing higher education that allowed her to persevere in all adversities and become a teacher's aide, working with students with behavioral issues and helping them achieve success in high school. Along the way, she and her husband also raised seven children and shared a happy life until she suffered a ministroke in 2015. The stroke led her to be depressed and rethink her position in life, including whether she should continue working or retire, and eventually she retired in 2015.

There is also a great lesson to be learned in how Mai Donohue dealt with depression after suffering a ministroke in 2015. Given her husband's health issues and now her own, she asked — as so many of us do — "Why me?" She felt useless, angry and disconnected from society. Even worse, she felt helpless until she sought help from a psychologist who helped her "get back on track." She realized there was "no magic pill" to solve her problems; it would take work to restore balance to her life. She also realized she had a decision to make: "Either I could be angry and unhappy for the rest of my life or grateful to be alive. I will fight for this gift with my last breath."

She decided to focus on the things in life that bring her joy — especially her passion for cooking. She further has aligned that passion with the larger purpose of helping others, as seen by using her 50th wedding anniversary celebration as a fundraiser. She cooked Vietnamese food for more than 200 guests and raised more than $1,000 for the Sophia Academy school for underprivileged girls in Providence.

With her renewed sense of confidence, she also ventured into writing her first book, a story *Crossing the Bamboo Bridge — Memoirs of a Bad Luck Girl.*

Mrs. Donohue is clearly enjoying life again, as evidenced in her words: "To keep myself emotionally and physically fit I wake up early every day and go to the YMCA and I treat it like a vacation not a workout. I travel to different cities and states to speak about my book and my life and try to inspire others to live their lives with joy and love. I continue to mentor students at Barrington High School with their senior projects. I invite my friends to lunch and dinners. This year we published a book of my husband's poetry, *The Night Watch Poems,* that he has been working on since before we met. I continue to support my three favorite charities, the Girl Scouts of Southeastern New England, the Sophia Academy and the Southeast Asian Community."

All of us, especially those of us who are seniors, can benefit by making aging our ally rather than treating it as a foe when adversity strikes. Here are two important lessons to be learned from Mrs. Donohue's incredible life story:

- We can make aging our closest ally by continuing to pursue our purposeful passions with unflinching determination and dedication.

- We must keep our mindset dynamic to search and pursue alternate passions if we encounter limitations or obstacles to pursuing a passion from earlier in life.

In the past 15 years of interacting with countless seniors, I have sadly observed that they don't realize their true passions and they lack a sense of purpose that could help make aging their ally and allow them to live a more productive and meaningful life, as Mai Donohue is doing. What is required is a serious reflection of our lives to recognize our passions – those things we love to do that give us gratification – as well as aligning them with a worthwhile purpose – a selfless act or acts that provide genuine personal happiness.

In the third section of this book, Five Mandates to Develop Your Dynamic Mindset, I will focus on reflection and ways to identify your true passions, which in turn can lead you to align them with the right purpose in your life.

If you can't figure out your purpose, figure out your passion. For your passion will lead you right into your purpose.
– T.D. Jakes, pastor, author, and filmmaker

Section 2

A Dynamic Mindset in Action

Chapter 9

Finding the Best

"Patience is bitter, but its fruit is sweet."

—Aristotle

Finding seniors who have assimilated most — if not all — of the beliefs of a dynamic mindset of aging was not an easy task. It took me more than two years to select who not only exemplified all five of the stringent criteria I set forth, but also have become my role models and mentors for the remaining years of my life. The five criteria are:

- Authenticity
- Accessibility
- Diversity
- Enthusiastic Engagement
- Inspirational Sharing

Authenticity

It is better to be an authentic loser than a false success,
and to die alive than to live dead.
— William Markiewicz,
author of *Extracts of Existence*

The first and foremost attribute of a worthy role model is that his or her life story is authentic and not fabricated to appear more impressive for personal gain. Without authenticity, everything else is meaningless. Authenticity manifests itself in the presence of comprehension, discovery and durability.

Comprehension: In the first three chapters, we categorically established that meaningful aging is a quest for happiness and that our mindset is the architect of the quality of our aging. Without a clear comprehension of these two overriding truths, any pursuit of meaningful aging is nothing more than wishful thinking. All five role models profiled in this book exhibit a high level of understanding of these truths.

Discovery: Meaningful aging is a personal pursuit; it must be discovered and not imitated. Discovery is only possible when we perceive the meaning of our aging simultaneously with our eyes, our minds and our hearts. In other words, using internal insight as well as external logic simultaneously provides us with an undistorted view of our aging – which helps us determine if it is indeed purposeful. All five role models featured here were driven to self-examination by adversity, natural curiosity or bafflement about their personal circumstances to assess their ongoing life journey based on their overall life experiences.

Durability: Meaningful aging is not a goal reached, but rather an ongoing journey. Achieving a desired goal is definitely a gratifying experience, including transitory pride or pleasure, but it does not necessarily result in lasting contentment. For someone to be a worthy role model of durable and meaningful aging, he or she exhibit evidence of maintaining a dynamic mindset of aging for at least five years after retirement. Each of the role models cited in this book have exhibited a dynamic mindset for 10 or more years and are thriving in their senior years because of it.

Accessibility

God does not ask your ability.

He asks only your availability.

—Mary Kay Ash,

founder of Mary Kay Cosmetics

It is common and tempting to quickly select our goals and ideals after reading a book or two by a particular author, or being mesmerized by the glittering success of a person, or even trusting the well-intentioned advice of a friend. Although these experiences may provide some valuable insights and guidance in our lives, relying on these external influences to determine the roadmap for our life's journey will likely end in disappointment. Until and unless we get inside the mind of a person and realistically grasp what is driving his or her mindset, it is difficult to determine whether that individual is worthy of becoming a role model for our journey of meaningful aging. We must have significant access to that person if we are to observe, reflect, interact and discuss the intricacies of his or her beliefs about aging.

It took me a long time — three years of observation, reflection, questioning and discussion — to identify five such role models from among the hundreds of people I've encountered in recent years. These five individuals provided remarkable accessibility, giving freely of their time to provide us with unblemished views of their aging.

Diversity

Diversity: the art of thinking independently together.

— Malcolm Forbes, entrepreneur

and publisher of Forbes magazine

Inspiring people and role models come in various forms and can be found among every part of society. They are not a special breed, but rather ordinary people like you and me. They are not the chosen few, bestowed with knowledge of a secret path to contentment, but instead are those who have used the power of common sense and the goodness of their hearts to understand and appreciate the true meaning of aging through constant learning and adapting to add meaning to their later years.

Since meaningful aging is a personal pursuit, we can't follow someone else's path to find personal contentment. What we can do is learn from other people and learn from them to devise our personal path to achieve contentment in the later years of our lives.

The five role models profiled in this section have achieved success and fulfillment in their personal, professional and retired lives. They also represent diverse cultural values and beliefs spanning the Americas, Europe, Asia and the Caribbean. These three men and two women ranging in age from the mid 60s to the late 80s, had professional backgrounds that ran the gamut: private industry, nonprofit organizations, education, journalism and medicine.

Enthusiastic Engagement

If you have zest and enthusiasm, you attract zest and enthusiasm.
Life does give you back in kind.
– Norman Vincent Peale, an American minister and author of the best-selling book *The Power of Positive Thinking*.

Another great trait of authentic role models is their enthusiastic engagement. Not only do they remain enthusiastically engaged in pursuing their own contentment, but they also show genuine and enthusiastic engagement with others who seek their wisdom in their personal journeys of ful-fillment.

In defining enthusiastic engagement, I decided that those featured as role models in this book must be able to reflect on their personal mindsets with respect to their personal journeys through life and be able to share those reflections in their own words and style in personal essays to be included here. By establishing these guidelines, I was able to share the stories of people who genuinely wanted to share their stories to help others and not just seek glory for themselves and their accomplishments.

Inspirational Sharing

Thousands of candles can be lighted from a single candle,
and the life of the candle will not be shortened.
Happiness never decreases by being shared.
— Buddha

The last but not least essential trait of an authentic role model is their will-ingness to share their dynamic mindset to inspire others, in essence making it contagious. By inspiring others to seek genuine happiness, they also ac-quire increased enthusiasm and energy for their own journey in aging.

Shared knowledge is accepted and effective only when it is believed to be logical and beneficial. This is how most of us decide whether to use the knowledge acquired from others when it comes to charting our own paths. But at times, even when it seems logical to accept such knowledge, our motivation to use it may wane over time.

To take advantage of this shared knowledge requires commitment-desire, determination and discipline. Commitment is a driving force that moves us towards our goal, but not to the end. What really gets us there is our inspiration, which requires both our commitment – desire, determination and discipline – and our devotion – enthusiasm, energy and affection. This powerful combination of two forces – commitment and devotion – provides inspiration and propels us to our goals. In order to take advantage of shared knowledge to sustain your motivation, you must convince your heart and mind to pursue your commitment and devotion to pursue meaningful aging.

In identifying role models of the dynamic mindset, this criteria of inspirational sharing weighed heavily on my mind. In my interactions with potential candidates, I was extremely interested in their mode of sharing information and whether their arguments had the power to inspire me and win both my logical and heartfelt acceptance.

Since I was fixated on these five essential attributes of meaningful aging when it came to selecting role models as examples of authenticity, accessibility, diversity, enthusiastic engagement and inspirational sharing, my search took longer than anticipated. It has been a long and rigorous journey for me, one that greatly tested my patience, perseverance and discipline. Nevertheless, it became a rewarding quest, as it has made my own retirement life more meaningful and joyful. So it is with utmost esteem and gratitude that I present to you my five role models of the dynamic mindset of meaningful aging:

- **Carol Young – A Do-gooder:** Prior to retiring in 2010 at age 67 from her hectic job as Deputy Executive Editor of Providence Journal –the oldest continuously published newspaper in the United States, she felt retirement would eliminate her sense of personal and professional identity. However, she quickly found a way to fill that void: In her amazing life after retirement, Ms. Young found an effective transition

114

from professional life to a meaningful life in retirement through her dynamic mindset of aging. At age 76, she is helping a half-dozen nonprofit organizations and is busier than ever with her multiple new roles.

- **Dr. Dinesh O. Shah – A Relentless Voyager:** An acclaimed scientist in the field of surface science engineering and nanotechnology and a beloved poet, at age 81 Dr. Shah is the retired head of the Chemical Engineering Department at the University of Florida in Gainesville, FL. Reflecting on his professional life made Dr. Shah aware of the fact that it was the power of his dynamic mindset that made him able to face serious adversities in his life and allowed him to achieve technical excellence and benevolence for others. Based upon that awareness, Dr. Shah has developed a 17-point code of conduct for a meaningful life in retirement. Following that code of conduct, he has been able to continue pursuing his passions of science and poetry and helping others.

- **Enrique Brouwer – A Cuban Gift:** Born in Havana, Cuba, and exiled to the Unites States as a refugee at age 15, Mr. Brouwer developed a dynamic mindset to achieve excellence and serve others by taking personal responsibility in every situation throughout his life. He made that dynamic mindset his life's mission – committed to pursuing harmony at home, excellence in work and service to others. The power of his dynamic mindset propelled him to become a distinguished corporate executive and educator in the United States. That dynamic mindset continues to serve him well in his early 70s as he continues to educate and help others in his retirement.

- **Vijaya Srinivasan— A Warrior Missionary.** A former long-term and subacute care regional administrator, Ms. Srinivasan faced death twice and, because of her dynamic mindset, not only survived those life-threatening experiences, but also is actively making a remarkable difference in the lives of many. At age 68, after surviving a double-lung transplant, Ms. Srinivasan is creating her legacy by helping other women to become self-sufficient by taking responsibility for their personal health and finances in their senior years. With the zeal of a warrior and the compassion of a missionary, she is ready to lend a helping hand to serve whenever and wherever she may be needed.

- **Dr. Thomas Mathew, MD – A Habitual Novice:** Born and educated as a medical doctor in Southern India, Dr. Mathew practiced anesthesiology in the United States and later founded an exotic spice farm and botanical garden in Belize, Central America. Dr. Mathew is a remarkable example of a dynamic mindset because of his commitment to constant learning, treating life as an adventure rather than an obligation and aligning his passions with a larger purpose of helping others.

In the ensuing five chapters, each one of these five role models will share their personal life stories of how they assimilated most, if not all of the five elements of the dynamic mindset of aging and are continuing the journey of their retirement lives with joyful contentment. At the end of each story will be a short analysis by me outlining the lessons which all of us can learn from their highly inspiring lives to make our own journey of retirement meaningful and delightful.

Chapter 10

A Do-gooder

Carol J. Young

Retired Deputy Executive Editor, Providence Journal

"I am a Do-gooder."

Hearing that unusual term from Carol Young, a longtime friend and colleague from Leadership Rhode Island, surprised me at first. However, my surprise quickly gave way to admiration for the sheer simplicity and sincerity of the term, which so aptly describes her.

I first met Carol in 2011, when we were both members of the advisory board of Leadership Rhode Island, a nationally recognized community leadership development organization in Providence, RI. She had retired the year before, after 45 years in journalism, including more than four decades as a reporter and editor at Rhode Island's largest newspaper, and she was continuing to serve the residents of Rhode Island in retirement, through her volunteer work at Leadership Rhode Island and other endeavors.

Even after I went on to become a member of the Board of Governors of Leadership Rhode Island in 2012 and had only occasional personal contact with Carol, I continued to witness the positive impact she had on the organization – and the entire state. She played a vital role at Leadership Rhode Island, where she not only edited the newsletter and other publications, as well as grants, but she also was always willing to lend a hand to anyone who needed help, from the youngest staff members to the executive director of the organization. Everyone held her in great esteem.

Intrigued by her commitment to volunteerism and the happiness she discovered in her self-described role as a do-gooder, I asked her to share her experiences of retirement life for this book, as an example for other seniors seeking to make their retirement lives productive and meaningful.

Here, in her own words, is her story.

My Discovery in the Golden Years

By Carol J. Young

On my last day of work on April 28, 2010, I walked into the Providence Journal newsroom to find everyone – reporters, photographers, editors and secretaries – wearing T-shirts with the slogan "Forever Young" dancing across the top. It was a day of sentimental speeches, witty tributes, gift presentations, lots of laughter and lots of cake. My 45-year career in newspapering was over. Just like that.

The decision to retire didn't come easily. I was consumed by my job; some would say overly so. For me, 12-hour workdays were routine, in part because news doesn't follow a 9-to-5 schedule. "News is the thing that happens when you make dinner plans," a colleague used to joke. Beyond that, there was *always* something more to do: another story to edit, phone calls to return, a chat with a reporter seeking advice.

I understood that retirement promised monumental change, a move away from the intense pressure of a newsroom into a deadline-free life-style. It also marked a move into a somewhat uncomfortable life of ano-nymity, a transition that would leave me with no status and no identity. After more than four decades of introducing myself first as Carol Young, Providence Journal reporter, and then, over the years, as state editor, city editor, metro desk editor, deputy executive editor, I would become Carol Young, nobody.

Nevertheless, I decided, at 67, that it was time to let go of an all-encompassing, all-consuming career and explore what retirement life had to offer.

When a reporter interviewed me about my pending retirement, I was asked the inevitable question: "What's next?" I blurted out that I was go-ing to learn to garden. I even bragged that I was going to have the most beautiful yard in my suburban town.

Truth be told, I had given no thought as to how I would fill the weeks, months and years ahead. I walked out the door of the Providence Journal that spring day of 2010 with one hope: that I would live up to that "For-ever Young" slogan on everyone's T-shirts for as long as humanly possi-ble.

On my first day of retirement, a longtime friend called to see how I was doing and to offer some well-meaning advice: "Don't say 'yes' to the first offers that come your way. Take time and figure out what you want to do," he advised.

I was confused. "Huh? What offers? I am not expecting anyone to reach out."

"Oh, you'll get calls," he predicted, noting that people would want to take advantage of my experience and prestige in the Rhode Island community.

Children are often asked: "What do you want to do when you grow up?" My friend urged me to confront a different version of that question: "What do you want to do now that you're retired?"

Whoa!

I sensed that I would *do* something and realized that the decision of *what to do* was mine to make. But at the time, I had no idea what that would be.

With the benefit of hindsight, my post-retirement journey, now in its ninth year, reflects the realization that I am happiest when I'm productive and harnessing my passions. You might say that I have unknowingly embraced elements both of the Dynamic Mindset and the Eternal Truths about Aging, concepts first introduced to me by my friend, Baldev Seekri, which he also outlined previously in this book.

Truth be told, much of what I do is downright selfish. I am obsessed with keeping my brain cells stimulated — if that is really possible. I also realized early in my retirement that I have a strong need to feel relevant.

However, neither of these issues dominated my thoughts during the spring and summer of 2010. I was focused solely on making good on my pledge to learn to garden.

My retirement ritual developed quickly: I woke between 8 and 9 a.m. and drank several cups of coffee while reading the morning newspaper.

For the first time in more than four decades, every story was a surprise because I had no part in producing any aspect of it.

Then, I would pull on shorts, a grubby shirt and sneakers and head out to my yard, where I happily spent 10 to 12 hours a day, digging up roots and removing overgrowth and boulders from an area destined to be the site of my first-ever garden. At dusk, sweaty and dirty, often sporting new blisters, I would pack away my tools and come inside to shower for dinner.

I completely underestimated how much I needed to learn about gardening. That was part of the attraction. At night, I'd search the internet or my new gardening books for answers to all kinds of questions: What insect is destroying my lily leaves? How do you compost? Which is better: chicken manure or horse manure?

I kept a garden journal in which I recorded each day's activities. "Picked my first cherry tomatoes — seven weeks after planting. Oh, so sweet!" I wrote one day. Failures were also noted. "The hydrangea in the front yard mystifies me. Got to find out why it won't flower. Too dry? Pruned wrong? Too much sun?"

During that first blissful summer, to my surprise, the overtures predicted by my friend actually materialized — long before I had figured out what I wanted to do. I rejected two proposals outright. Three others forced me to do some serious thinking.

The first came in a letter I received on July 1 from David Dooley, president of the University of Rhode Island, in which he invited me to join the President's Advisory Council at URI. Serving on the council struck me as an intriguing use of time, mostly because I have had a longtime interest in higher education, especially in Rhode Island's public colleges and university. Yet, I was hesitant to accept.

I spent time trying to understand the source of my reluctance. The more I thought about it, the more it became clear that my hesitation was tied to my former role as "Carol Young – journalist." I had spent my working life in a newsroom, where reporters and editors learn from the get-go that they are observers – never participants, never advocates and never advisors.

Realization One: I must change my mindset if I am going to find a purposeful role in this, the final chapter, of my life.

In a letter to President Dooley accepting the invitation, I acknowledged my angst. "After a 45-year career in a profession that required me to behave as a neutral, impartial observer in all public policy debates, I may struggle in a new role of openly expressing opinions and recommendations, but I am certainly willing to try."

At about the same time, I heard from Mike Ritz, then the newly appointed executive director of Leadership Rhode Island (LRI), an organization that inspires leaders in the private, public and non-profit sectors of Rhode Island to work for the greater good of the community. "Want to meet for coffee?" he asked. Thinking that he wanted to meet some of the program's 2000 alumni — I had participated in the organization's 10-month leadership program in 1992 — I agreed to meet him at a bakery in Providence. We had a nice chat.

Turns out Mike was doing some *reconnaissance,* taking stock of my inclinations and interests *in assisting the organization.* A few weeks later, he called again, this time with a specific request: Would I co-chair the Leadership Rhode Island program for the upcoming Class of 2011? Co-chairs participate in planning meetings to help design the curriculum for each month's theme (education, criminal justice, economy to name three). Co-chairs also attend the orientation retreat for members of the incoming class, their 10 day-long class sessions and their class graduation.

"That sounds like work. Let me think about it," I said, secretly hoping he'd find some other alum to do the job instead.

In late summer, I was outside doing battle with weeds when my husband hollered out to me that I had a phone call. Turns out, Mike Ritz was as persistent as the dandelions and crabgrass. "OK. You've had time to think. Will you be co-chair?" he asked. I sought a few more details about the demands of the role and then appealed for "just a little more time" to decide.

Thoughts rolled around in my head as I resumed weeding: *To do this right, you will have to keep up with all the big issues facing Rhode Island . . . You will be giving up a sizable chunk of your newly gained free time . . .*

Then I had the scariest thought of all: *How will you fill your days this fall and winter, when you have no garden to tend?*

I called Mike to say yes.

Realization Two: I will thrive if I remain involved with people who are upbeat and committed to improving the larger community.

A third overture came from Terri Adelman, then the executive director of Inspiring Minds, a nonprofit organization in Providence, RI, that sends hundreds of volunteer tutors into classrooms throughout the city to work one-on-one with children struggling to learn. During my early days as a reporter in the 1960s, I had written stories about the feisty women who had started the tutorial program and, over the years, I had kept tabs on the organization as it expanded its services throughout the city of Providence. I also quietly contributed to its annual appeal.

Inspiring Minds volunteer tutoring a student

At lunch one sunny afternoon, Terri described plans to concentrate the organization's tutoring efforts on the earliest grades, kindergarten to third grade, where the impact could be the greatest. "Are you in?" she asked. "Sure," I said, not really knowing whether she was looking for my time, treasure or talent.

Turns out she was looking for all three. That *yes* led to a nine-year association with Inspiring Minds, during which I organized several fundraising events, assisted in public relations and served as secretary and chair of the Board of Directors.

I have always believed that a solid education is a ticket to success in life; it is the great leveler, giving all children a chance to succeed, regardless of the color of their skin, their native language, or the income of their families.

Chairperson Carol Young, Inspiring Minds showing off the award trophy for the potential winner of outdoor Trivia Night fundraiser in 2018.

Realization Three: Happiness comes when you find constructive ways to incorporate your passions into your daily life.

By the end of my first year of retirement, I was fully engaged with three very different nonprofit organizations and had smaller roles with two others.

What attracted me to volunteer work? That's a seemingly obvious question that, until now, I had no particular need to answer. Clearly there is more than one explanation. I've come up with several.

The Pompous Answer: I have had a comfortable life and it is time to give back. Work-for-pay carries obligations and limits flexibility. Volunteering is serious business, too, but you are more likely to be doing what you want to do when you want to do it. Though it sounds corny, the compensation comes in personal satisfaction, not dollars. Because of my all-in personality, volunteering has actually restricted the flexibility often associated with retirement. "You're busier now than when you were working," my husband mutters, as I run out the door for a meeting or when he sees me in front of the computer, working late into the night on one of my volunteer projects.

The Smart Aleck Answer: If someone asks for help, I can't say no. Just recently, while serving on a jury at the Rhode Island Superior Court, I had lunch with another juror, a young woman who serves as a college counselor at a charter high school serving disadvantaged teens. On the final day of the trial, when the 12 of us reached a verdict and were saying good-bye, the young professional called me aside with a question: Would I be willing to help some of her students with their essays for college applications? "I'd love to," I said, without taking a minute to consider how I would manage to do that, given my jam-packed calendar.

Sometimes I don't wait to be asked. An offer to help rolls off my tongue with ease. I discovered, while chatting with a high school classmate at our 55th reunion, that he was writing his memoirs. "Wow! Send me what you've written," I said. He did. I could see that he had a compelling life story to tell, one that would be considerably better at the hands of an editor. "It's great," I told him. "Want me to edit it?"

For more than two years, my classmate and I, who live 1,700 miles away have exchanged hundreds of emails and phone calls and tons of laughter as we've rewritten the story of his life, chapter by chapter. His wit, his ability to recall scenes and interactions from decades ago, and his willingness to write about his life's highs and lows, combine to create an extraordinary story about a seemingly ordinary life.

The Selfish Answer: I want to keep my brain in overdrive. "Aging is about living, not ceasing to live," Baldev writes, in an earlier section of this book. Taking great liberties, I would add this corollary: "Aging is about thinking, not ceasing to think." I don't know if there is any scientific basis to the old axiom, *Use It or Lose It,* but common sense suggests that retirement is not the time to give your brain or your body — a rest. Reaching out for new responsibilities, new experiences and new challenges is a deliberate effort to continually exercise my brain.

Here is just one example:

After co-chairing a few major fundraising events for the non-profit educational organization Inspiring Minds, I argued that we could increase the proceeds from the annual silent auction, an integral part of our traditional chicken dinner events, by expanding the bidding pool to people who were not able or did not want to attend the event.

The idea of potentially raising more money by inviting outside bids understandably had plenty of support, but no one on the staff had the time or inclination to learn how to use an online bidding service. The burden of creating this new venture rested with me, a *bona fide* technophobe.

I spent long hours over several days in trial and error, stoically studying the directions, reminiscent of the way I once studied a foreign language. "This isn't rocket science," I sputtered, to myself. "If others can do this, so can you."

When everything finally clicked and I had mastered the online program, I celebrated privately. I had learned something I had doubted I could. It turned out to be a victory for Inspiring Minds, too. The proceeds from our silent auction increased dramatically as a result of the additional bids.

The Goody Two-shoes Answer: I am happiest when I am doing something I consider meaningful. Let's be clear: I love picking a home-grown tomato off the vine, cheering for my daughter as she crosses the finish line of a marathon, and traveling to faraway places on family vacations. However, a life filled with personal pleasures is not enough for me.

I acknowledge the subjective nature of *meaningful*. Running for political office, babysitting one's grandchildren, leading a campaign to save pollinating bees from extinction, or taking a lonely friend out to the movies are all purposeful activities. I pursue volunteer endeavors that are meaningful for me.

A key reason I value my continuing association with Leadership Rhode Island is that the organization's core mission is to encourage its graduates to lead in whatever way they chose to improve the larger community.

After co-chairing the year-long leadership class in 2011, I remained active with the organization by participating in fundraising phone-a-thons, interviewing applicants for upcoming classes and serving on various advisory committees.

My most useful contributions draw on the skills developed in my newspaper career. Working with staff members and talented volunteers, we produce an amazingly interesting and informative newsletter. I also had a key role in the production of two of the organization's books and serve as the on-call editor for many of its other publications.

For someone who views newspaper journalism as a public service, it naturally follows that I would view my many editing projects for different organizations as meaningful activities during my retirement. That's why I willingly share editing responsibilities for a blog produced by a retired Providence Journal reporter who is covering Rhode Island's efforts to comply with a federal order to overhaul services for thousands of developmentally disabled residents.

The Needy Answer: I shudder to even say this, but I need to feel appreciated. The twilight years can be depressing, a period when one can easily begin to feel useless, out-of-touch, irrelevant. It has been my experience that nonprofit organizations, often under-financed and under-staffed, enthusiastically welcome volunteers willing to offer their time and skills to help them fulfill their missions. In return, the volunteer is rewarded by feeling useful and needed.

Sometimes there's an even greater payoff. Most leaders of the non-profit organizations I have encountered go out of their way to show their appreciation. It's a gift I didn't expect and one I didn't even know I needed. Yet, in hindsight, the more appreciation I have received for my volunteer work, the more eager I am to contribute.

Carol Young talking to former Rhode Island Governor Lincoln Chafee after receiving Leadership Rhode Island's Inspiring Leaders Volunteer Award on March 17, 2013

Filling the identity gap loomed large when I first retired, but its importance faded over the years. That's probably because I filled the void, without thinking about it. Here's how I know:

At a recent meeting of the URI President's Advisory Council, the two dozen individuals in attendance, many of them executives and business owners, were asked to introduce themselves. When my turn came, I made a fleeting reference to my earlier life as a Providence Journal editor and then said, with a smile, "I now spend my time as a 'do-gooder." I was pleasantly surprised that the mention of my new role drew warm smiles from others at the table.

Relevance and Dynamic Mindset in Senior Years

*"We forget that **old** in age typically does not mean*
***old** in terms of relevance."*
—Craig D. Lounsbrough,
author of *The Eighth Page*

Carol Young's journey of retirement highlights two important aspects of aging: the need for relevance and the power of having a dynamic mindset.

As seniors, we can learn from her retirement experience to make our current or impending retirement life more exciting and meaningful.

Relevance in Aging: The human need to feel relevant — recognized and appreciated — is always with us, but it's even more intense in our advanced years. If we don't feel relevant, we may perceive ourselves as useless and burdensome for others. Prior to retirement, most people spend a lot of time planning for financial and physical stability, however, they often ignore their emotional needs — especially a sense of relevance in identity and purpose.

Unlike most people who start their retirement journey ignorant of the most demanding challenges they are going to face, Carol Young recognized this in her following statement:

I understood that retirement promised monumental change, a move away from the intense pressure of a newsroom into a deadline-free lifestyle. It also marked a move into a life of anonymity, a transition that would leave me with no status and no identity. After more than four decades of introducing myself first as Carol Young, Providence Journal reporter, and then, over the years, as state editor, city editor, metro desk editor, deputy executive editor, I would become Carol Young, nobody.

Carol recognized the void of relevance she would be experiencing, but had no idea at the time how she would fill that void. This brings us to the second aspect—the discovery of her dynamic mindset of aging.

Dynamic Mindset of Aging: Switching from gardening to volunteering for numerous nonprofit organizations, Carol gradually and unknowingly realized and embraced the dynamic mindset of aging, as seen in her following statement:

"With the benefit of hindsight, my post-retirement journey, now in its ninth year, reflects the realization that I am happiest when I'm productive and harnessing my passions. You might say that I have unknowingly embraced elements both of the Dynamic Mindset and the Eternal Truths about Aging, concepts introduced earlier in this book by my friend, Baldev Seekri, which he also outlined previously in this book."

The key elements of the dynamic mindset of aging are quite vivid in her following three realizations:

- I must change my mindset if I am going to find a purposeful role in this, the final chapter, of life.
- I will thrive if I remain involved with people who are upbeat and committed to improving the larger community.
- Happiness comes when you find constructive ways to incorporate your passions into your daily life.

The gist of the above three realizations is at the core of the dynamic mindset of aging during our senior years, which is to seek happiness by continual learning and to take responsibility of aligning our passions with a larger purpose of helping others.

After nine years into her satisfying retirement journey, Carol Young has become a great example of the dynamic mindset and has adapted to her life as a happy and satisfied retiree, willing to learn new skills and share her knowledge with others through volunteerism.

When asked why volunteerism became her medium to display her dynamic mindset, she offered a number of explanations before revealing the genuine answer: "I shudder to even say this, but I need to feel appreciated. The twilight years can be depressing, a period when one can easily begin to feel useless, out-of-touch, irrelevant. It has been my experience that nonprofit organizations, often under-financed and understaffed, enthusiastically welcome volunteers willing to offer their time and skills to help them fulfill their missions. In return, the volunteer is rewarded by feeling useful and needed."

Volunteering has given Carol relevance in retirement, allowing her to create a new identity that she's had all along: a do-gooder.

"Aging is an extraordinary process where you become the person you always should have been."
—David Bowie,
British singer, songwriter and actor

Chapter 11

A Relentless Voyager

Dinesh O. Shah

Scientist by Profession and Poet at Heart

Professor Emeritus at the University of Florida

"Dr. Shah, when you have time, can you please express your sentiments about aging in poetry?"

It was a nice October day in 2018. We had just finished lunch in the communal dining room and were chatting about my plans to write my next book about aging. Dr. Shah beamed with his distinctive smile, indicating his willingness to oblige me.

At the time, Dr. Shah was the president of the Shantiniketan 2 Condominium Association in Tavares, FL, and was in the midst of resolving a very serious issue concerning the food club supplier and working on his editorial write-up for his latest invention — a chemical treatment designed to help soil retain more water potentially increasing crop production throughout the world. That article was to be published in the November 2018 issue of *The International Journal of Agriculture and Food Technology.* Understanding his preoccupation with these projects, I didn't expect to receive a poem from him for weeks. The next morning, I was pleasantly surprised to find three copies of his poem in my mailbox, one in Gujarati, Dr. Shah's native language, one in Hindi, the official language of India, and one in English. Here is the English version:

THE DAWN OF OLD AGE

*The night of my youth has gone and now
the dawn of old age has arrived!
I've tumbled many times in my life, but
now I know to walk carefully
No one knows the secret of what has given me the deep brown color
Like henna when crushed between two
stones, gets its deep brown color
I have spoken a lot in my past; now the
time has come for me to listen
I never thought about why I came to planet Earth, but now I do think of it
In the farm of my life, many good people
have planted the seeds of wisdom
This is only a rest stop, looking over the
serene lake of memories
Fold up your tent and pack up your stuff
is the order from God
But I want to see the path travelled from
the top of the mountain peak*

MEANINGFUL AGING

In sands of memories, some people have
left their footprints forever
And at this dawn, I am putting my own
footprints in this sand.

The very first line of his poem, describing the beginning of old age the dawn of life rather than the onset of sunset, envisioned by most seniors and adults alike, exponentially increased my zeal to write this book. His words brilliantly captured the essential elements of a dynamic aging mindset that I had in mind to propagate among other seniors. I decided to get to know Dr. Shah more, so I could really understand his philosophy of life.

Meet 81-year-young Dr. Dinesh O. Shah, a current resident of the Shantiniketan retirement community and retired head of the department of Chemical Engineering at the University of Florida in Gainesville, FL. Dr. Shah is one of the most commonly cited scientists in publications about surface science, engineering and nanotechnology. During his career of over 40 years in chemical engineering, he had been invited to more than 100 corporate research centers to provide consulting services to a variety of technical problems and has presented more than 300 seminars in his areas of expertise. Dr. Shah also provided consulting services to large corporations such as Alcoa, Alcon, Procter & Gamble, Kraft Food, Akzo Nobel, PPG Industries, Sun Oil Company, and others in the United States and India. In his hometown of Kapadwanj, India, a road was named **International Scientist Dr. Dinesh O. Shah Road** to honor his lifelong contributions to education and research.

Dr. Shah was also active outside of pursuing his own research, spearheading a project to raise $1 million to build the India Cultural and Education Center (ICEC) at the University of Florida in Gainesville, FL. Additionally, Dr. Shah established an award for the best PhD thesis in surface and colloid science in India, and he helped establish the Shah-Schulman Center for Surface

135

Science and Nanotechnology at Dharmsinh Desai-University in Nadiad, India, with the joint support of the government, industry and the university. Dr. Shah also established the D.O. Shah Annual Lecture in Surface Science at the University of Florida, which allows prominent researchers to offer presentations on breakthroughs in the field of surface science. The list goes on...

Along with pursuing his incredible career in academia, Dr. Shah not only kept his passion of writing poetry alive, but further enhanced it by partnering with Kartik Trivedi, the world-renowned painter whose paintings hang in the White House, Buckingham Palace, and French National Art Gallery. Dr. Shah would send his poems to Mr. Trivedi, who would in turn create pencil drawings, capturing the sentiments of the verses. Once Dr. Shah approved the pencil drawings, Mr. Trivedi would begin a painting based on the sketch. The following is one of many of those paintings:

A painting by Kartik Trivedi, based upon Dr. Shah's poem Panihari
(women fetching water)

The more I learned about Dr. Shah's remarkable past of relentlessly pursuing his seemingly disparate passions of science and poetry to positively impact many lives, the more I wanted to learn about his philosophy of life and his plans for the balance of his golden years. Despite his busy schedule, Dr. Shah agreed to share his mindset about life and his plans to continue the journey into the most important phase of his life with vigor and positive anticipation. Here is Dr. Shah's vision in his own words:

The Game of My Life

By Dinesh O. Shah

"I do not want your money, but I would greatly appreciate you coming here for a few months every year and spending time with my young faculty and students to encourage their research on surface science and nanotechnology."

Hearing those words from Dr. Sudhir Jain, Director of the Indian Institute of Technology (IIT) in Gandhinagar, Western India, I felt a surge of energy rushing through my body, making me feel like a young man at age 81. Expounding on his request, which came in response to my offer of a significant donation to IIT, Dr. Jain continued, "Dr. Shah, this is like the story of the Kauravas and Pandavas, the two parties involved in the Kurukshetra War in India around 1000 BCE. Both sides — Pandavas and Kauravas — approached Lord Krishna for help. Lord Krishna declared that one side could take his entire army, and the other could take him though he would not fight. Dharyodan, the chieftain of Kauravas took Lord Krishna's army, while Arjuna, the chieftain of Pandavas, took Lord Krishna. Arjuna told Lord Krishna, 'I do not want your army, but I would greatly appreciate if you would come with me.' And, as we know, Arjuna's Pandavas defeated the Kauravas badly. This is exactly what I am trying to say.

Your money would certainly help the institute and its students, but your presence here for a few months every year will be invaluable to inspire countless students and faculty for generations to come. Not only will it stimulate their minds for research in surface science and nanotechnology, but it also will give them a rare chance of witnessing the display of the tenacity and genius of the human spirit at its best."

Tears of contentment and gratitude rolled down my cheeks as I listened to Dr. Jain. I found myself awestruck and speechless.

Writing poetry puts me on cloud Nine

I have been writing poems and songs since I was in sixth grade. I write for my own enjoyment. Each poem feels like an encapsulation of my emotions, and when a composer selects the appropriate melody and a singer sings with the appropriate voice, the audience is able to experience those feelings. It also gives me the feeling that I am on cloud number nine. I keep listening to that song again and again – maybe more than 50 times. I really appreciate the talents of the composers, singers, and musicians — they give my poetry its soul.

The Lamps of humanity song is one of my favorites. This song based upon my poem was composed and sung by well-known composer Ashit Desai in Mumbai, India and was presented during a concert at Parab Tara Pani in 1986. It has a lot of science in it; it even has a structure like science, e.g., observation, asking the question and finding the answer! Like the great scientist Isaac Newton, who saw an apple falling to the ground from a tree. He asked the question, "Why did it come down and not go up or sideways?" and then he found the answer in the laws of gravity. This song has that type of structure."

138

LAMPS OF HUMANITY

Composer and Singer Ashit Desai sings Lamps of Humanity at
Bharatiya Vidya Bhavan, Mumbai, India, in 1986

A star falls from the sky in a moment, leaving behind a trail of light
A firefly keeps on flying with its pulsating light

An incense stick burns within a few minutes, but the fragrance lingers on
The earthen lamp burns until the end of the night

The lightening lasts as long as the thunderstorm lasts
The moonlight lasts until the arrival of dawn

Somewhere I have read that the Universe is finite
And after ages, the sun will cool down

O' Great Architect of the Universe, how come you made this
great mistake
That you did not make a lamp that can shine forever?
Someone replied from the sky: 'Yes, I made such lamps and put
one in everyone's heart
If lighted they can illuminate the whole Universe!
It is these lamps of humanity, which are lit by the spark of love
and compassion
That shall shine forever like Buddha, Jesus, Teresa and Gandhi!

My dear friend Mr. Baldev Seekri asked that I explain how, like a relentless voyager, I have the energy to both pursue my own passions while also making sure I give others. His inquiry caused me to reflect on moments like my conversation with Dr. Jain in IIT episode in Gandhinagar and the 1986 concert in Mumbai and it became quite clear to me that my ceaseless efforts to pursue my passions of science and poetry and to make them enablers to inspire and help others are not ascribed to any secret or formula, but are products of the mindset with which I have played and continue to play the game of my life. So, I thought of no better way to talk about my life through the analogy of a football game.

Is Life Similar to a Football Game?

Having been born and raised in India, I came to the United States at age 23 and did not know anything about the American game of football. I could not understand while watching this game on TV why players used to push and pile onto each other. However, over time, and with the help of a few friends, I began to understand it —The game is divided into four quarters of 15 minutes each. The last quarter is most exciting if the two teams are less than seven points apart. I see a tremendous similarity between this game and life. In football, the quarterback must be quick, decisive, and accurate in action and focus. **We are quarterbacks in the game of life.**

Similarly, in Indian culture, we also traditionally divide life into four quarters, each one 25 years long, assuming that a healthy individual should live to be 100 years old. The first quarter is marked by childhood and student life. In the second quarter, we experience married life, and the joy of starting a family. In the third quarter, we serve our families, our communities, and the needy. And, finally, in the last quarter of our lives, we focus on detachment and salvation, Moksha and Nirvana. In this article, I will briefly describe how my first three quarters have gone, and then focus on the fourth quarter and what I would like to do with this – the final and most important quarter of my life.

I was born on March 31, 1938, in Mumbai, and we moved to our ancestral town of of Kapadwanj in Gujrat state of India when I was four years old. Growing up, my family faced significant financial hurdles, especially following the passing of my father when I was only nine years old. I lived with my mother, my two older sisters, and my two younger brothers. In India at the time, it was unconventional for widows to join the workforce, and I found myself shouldering much of the financial burden at a young age. I began taking up odd jobs, and between cleaning my own school building after classes, painting greeting cards, doing farm work, and tutoring children, I was able to support my family. My mother's name was Shardaben, which translates to "Goddess of Knowledge." She was always kind and supportive, even through our family's hardest times. Throughout my childhood, she emphasized the importance of education, and she even sold her jewelry to pay college fees for me and my siblings. She led us by example, most notably showing us that our lives are our

141

own responsibility, and we should live them without complaint. It is this lesson that inspired me and continues to motivate me, becoming an integral element of my mindset throughout life.

After completing high school, I attended Mumbai University for my college education and received a Bachelor of Science Degree in Physics and Mathematics, and a Master of Science Degree in Biophysics. In 1961, left for New York City and attended Columbia University, where I earned my Ph.D. in Biophysics. This completed the first quarter of my life, from 1938 through 1963.

In the second quarter of my life, I met my wife, Suvarna, who had also come to the United States from India to earn her Ph. D. in Statistics. She had the same cultural and family background as me, and our mutual attraction to one another ultimately culminated in our marriage at Columbia University. I then spent one year with NASA in their Exobiology Division, and two years at Columbia University doing oceanography work. In 1970, I joined the University of Florida as a joint faculty member in the Anesthesiology and Chemical Engineering Departments despite my lack of formal training in these fields. Within five years, I became a full professor, which usually takes anywhere from ten to fourteen years. Eventually, I was appointed as the chairman of the department. While I was advancing in my career, Suvarna and I had a daughter and a son in 1969 and 1971 respectively. And, with the birth of my children and appointment as chairman, I had completed the second quarter of my life from 1963 through 1988.

As the third quarter of my life began, I was diagnosed with late onset of Type 1 Diabetes. At the same time, I was honored by the University of Florida with an endowed chair, becoming the first Charles Stokes Professor of Chemical Engineering and Anesthesiology. Shortly after, in 2000, my beloved wife passed away due to a brain tumor. In 2007, I retired as

I wanted free time to pursue my dreams. Primarily, I wanted to spend more time with my children and grandchildren. Additionally, I felt that the Indian government, and my community had spent money to educate me from first grade to my master of science degree, but I had not paid them back in any form.

Consequently, I decided to spend six months performing volunteer work in India every year. I selected a small university in Gujarat, Dharmsinh Desai University (DDU), and decided to set up a modern research facility dedicated to the study of surface science and nanotechnology, which I specialized in. At the end of 2007, I had submitted a proposal to Gujarat Govt to establish a Surface Science and Nanotechnology center. The Current Prime Minister of India Mr. Narendra Modi, who was the Chief Minister of Gujarat at that time invited me and my colleagues to discuss the project.

Prime Minister Narindera Modi (left) and me in 2008

Mr. Modi asked many exploratory questions about how this Center can help Industry and was quite satisfied with our answers. After four days of that meeting, I received a letter from Gujarat Govt that they have approved 3.5 crore rupees for the Center and subsequently, I received the check.. This center was one of the first project involving Government, University and ten major companies. With that necessary financing, I was able to establish a state-of-the-art research center. I personally trained ten Ph.D. students and six faculty members, and between 2007 and 2017, I published 45 research papers in international journals. And as 2013 came to a close, so did the third quarter of my life, from 1988 through 2013.

Currently, I am in my sixth year of my final quarter. I live in a retirement community in Tavares, FL, with other retired Indian professionals who immigrated to the United States in the 60s and 70s. This community is about 88 miles from Gainesville, where I had lived for 48 years. Among residents of this community I met very inspiring friends, including Baldev Seekri, and the writing of this chapter is a testimonial to his encouragement. It is obvious that any person in the fourth quarter would think about what he or she would like to do with their remaining time. I am no exception!

I have already made a list of books, both regarding science and poetry, that I would like to complete in this final quarter, including my biography for my grandchildren and the world. Further, I have identified a few qualities that might help anyone who wants to remain in good mental and physical health while also maintaining a high level of productivity. The following points are guides or codes to help me stay focused, inspired, and resolute — and, hopefully, win the game in the fourth quarter.

- Demonstrate enthusiasm for doing things. Keep yourself busy. Always think of identifiable outcomes of your work.

- Serve the society in any way possible. As Baldev Seekri says, give your 3 T's – time, talent and treasure.

- Adore and guide your grandchildren — they are at least 25% your own genes! I wrote a storybook called *Walking with my Dada* with my grandson, Avan, in which he retold and illustrated stories from my childhood. We sold the book through Amazon, and all of the proceeds go to the North-South Foundation charity, which helps educate underprivileged Indian children.

- Show compassion for others. The Hindu poet-saint Tulsidas wrote the following: *Compassion is the root of all religions and ego is the foundation of all sins!*

- Learn to forgive and forget the bad deeds committed against you. Do not curse others for their actions, but thank God that you are not doing those actions.

- Stay positive. If you must dwell on the past, think of the best events and not the painful or miserable events. In one of my poems, I wrote: *I love my memories more than the diamonds and jewels. And therefore, my true wealth is hidden in my memories.*

- Do good deeds. The Indian mystic and poet Kabir wrote: *When you came to this world as an infant, you were crying and the world was rejoicing. Now live your life in such a manner, that when you leave this world, you go smiling and the world is crying.* The fourth quarter is your last chance to do good deeds for the people around you.

- Focus on yourself and your deeds, not on others and their deeds.

- Identify and appreciate your good karma of the bygone years. Do not expect anything in return when you do good to another person.

- Include modest but regular exercise in your routine, such as walking or performing yoga exercises.

- Remove ego when you help others. Remember that God gave you extra so that you may share with others.

- Do what your own conscience tells you, and not what other people say.

- Have dreams to do good karma in the coming days, months and years. Not all dreams may become reality, but some do. I wrote in one of my poems: *I am moving forward with dreams of a long journey. When I get tired, I take a rest for a while!*

- Leave behind a positive example for your grandchildren to follow. We are the role models for coming generations.

- Try to become a bridge that connects individuals, nations, and cultures.

- Be a catalyst to promote good activities or projects.

- Leave behind a legacy of a world made better by your sincere efforts.

In my fourth and final quarter, I decided to invest my time and energy in my own community, having been elected president of the condominium association. I had made it very clear that I would hold this position for only one year. My term ended on December 31, 2018. In early December, we arranged a tour of eight countries of Central America for 50 of the residents through Norwegian Cruise Lines. That trip brought the residents closer to each other, like a family, and I feel good that I was able to improve the lives of my fellow residents.

I now hope to focus on my books of poetry as well as manuscripts related to nanotechnology and surface science in the coming months. I appropriately wrote in one of my poems the followings:

The night is short, but I want to count all the stars

My destination is far away, but I want to reach there on my feet!

As with a football game, I am hoping that this final quarter of my

life will end in a roaring touchdown!

— Dinesh O. Shah,

ShantiNiketan 2, Tavares, FL 32778

Aging is Living

Dr. Shah's mindset about life is a great example for young and the old alike. His achievements before and after retirement are a testimony to the eternal truth that aging, at any stage of life, is about living and not for ceasing to live, as most people mistakenly start to believe as they enter the final quarter of their game. His game of life continues unabated with increasing enthusiasm and positive anticipation for the future.

Some may declare Dr. Shah's incredible success as a matter of luck, thinking his life has been smooth sailing. But the reality is far from this misconception. Dr. Shah's life hasn't been a bed of roses, but rather a series of challenges that have tested his resolve and fortitude to survive and thrive. The challenges of losing his father at the tender age of nine, his financial hardships during his school years, the loss of his beloved wife from cancer, and facing Late Onset of Type 1 Diabetes are some of the many impediments that could have broken his will to live, let alone achieve such success. But the values Dr. Shah learned from his mother helped forge his dynamic mindset of taking responsibility for his circumstances; sculpting a better quality of life with his efforts and continual learning; discovering and pursuing his passions of science and poetry and using them to help humanity; and demonstrating an unflinching belief in the continuity of life to make his human existence meaningful. That dynamic mindset not only propelled him to the pinnacle of

147

success, but is also making the last quarter of his life the dawn of hope and optimism for more good things to come.

For the balance years of his life, as articulated in his write-up, Dr. Shah has prepared a manifesto of 17 codes of conduct to keep him focused, inspired and disciplined. These codes direct him to serve society at large by giving his 3T's — time, talent and treasure to the needy; to adore and guide the next generation— his grandchildren; to become a unifying force for mankind; to pursue his passions of science and poetry; and most importantly to leave his legacy of excellence and benevolence for the benefit of others.

When asked what it takes to be a person like Dr. Shah, Dr. P. A. Joshi, the current chairman of Anchor Technologies in India who worked with Dr. Shah for 11 years to establish the Nanotechnology Center in India responded: "Be a selfless, humble and untiring person with a passion to do whatever possible for the betterment of society with a positive humanitarian attitude."

By seeing aging as a part of his game, rather than the dreaded nightmare, that many seniors do, Dr. Shah continues to play the final quarter of life and is able to live his life with the zeal of a relentless voyager seeking to achieve fulfillment for himself and making the lives of those around him better. In the process of doing so, he reminds all of us about the following commonly forgotten lesson for mankind:

The meaning of life is to find your gift,
and the purpose of life is to give it away.
—Pablo Picasso

Chapter 12

A Cuban Gift – Noblesse Oblige

Enrique J. Brouwer

Managing Director, Brouwer Executive Coaching International, LLC

Portland, Oregon

"My mission in life is to create harmony at home,
achieve excellence in work and provide service to others.
To the degree that I do, I consider myself a success."
—Enrique Brouwer

The above statement was a game changer for me.

In 2014, three years after publishing my first book, *Organizational Turnarounds with a Human Touch*, I was thinking about writing a second book about success. During the exploratory stage, I posed a question – *What does success mean to you?* – to 15,000 members of the Integrated Leadership and Change Management Group on LinkedIn, a social networking site for professionals. Most of the responses I received centered around achieving goals and winning.

In contrast to those responses, the enunciation of personal success by Enrique Brouwer, a former educator at Washington State University in Vancouver, WA, and a retired corporate executive and consultant, stood apart and touched my heart unlike anything I had experienced before. Not only had he clearly defined his vision of personal success, but he also used that definition as his life's mission.

Enrique's articulation of how he measures personal success greatly inspired me and helped transform my vague thoughts about writing the book into a firm commitment to do so. At the same time, it also made me want to learn more about him and his philosophy of life. I read more of his inspiring views about life, success and happiness in various articles he wrote and the comments he posted in group discussions on LinkedIn. As I did so, my curiosity increased to such a degree that I reached out to him. "Your definition of success is definitely going to be a part of my book," I wrote. "Also, as I proceed further with my exploration of this intriguing subject of success, I will be coming back to you for your wisdom and advice."

He responded to my message almost immediately. "I am touched by your attention and remain at your service in any way necessary," he wrote. "I leave you with the Cuban wish for friends: *Un abrazo* — a hug to you."

In the ensuing weeks and months, as we shared information about our professional and personal lives with each other through emails and exchanged ideas on assorted topics by participating in a variety of group discussions on LinkedIn, we developed a high degree of mutual respect and admiration for one another. I asked Enrique if he would share his life story — not just his definition of success, but also his views as to the mindset needed to achieve success — for inclusion in my upcoming book. He graciously agreed.

His story, explaining how he learned the true meaning of personal success while living in a refugee camp in Florida after being exiled from Cuba at age 15, was titled *From Cuba with Love*. It was so powerful that I not only used it in my book, *Seizing Success — How Mindset Makes It Happen*, but also as a model for six other people who contributed their stories for that book. It also generated a positive response and widespread praise from readers once the book was published.

Over the past five years, our relationship has evolved from being strangers into becoming cherished pals and we frequently share our opinions on various subjects and seek advice from each other on various matters.

So, it was natural that I would ask Enrique, who is now 72 and retired, to offer his thoughts as to his mindset for meaningful aging, which are presented here.

Meaningful Aging

By Enrique J. Brouwer

I retired in May 2017, after six years of teaching at Washington State University in Vancouver. Prior to that, I worked for 30 years in the corporate world. My success in those times was measured by organizational goals and the achievement of my goals in serving others. My personal mission statement is: *Harmony at home, excellence in work and service to others.*

After a period of serious reflection, I realized that, over time, I have gained perspectives that allow me to not only ponder the learning accomplished on the road traveled to date, but also to look towards the horizon and relish the road ahead. In a short poem, I aimed to capture the benefits of perspective as an analytical tool. My analysis tends to the lyrical, but it is analysis nonetheless.

Words in Amber

Like ancient ants caught in amber
Words hang suspended in a poem
Trapped in grammatical resin
Preserved feelings in suspension
Safe to be examined from all angles
Neither sting nor joy, but silhouettes of
bygone memories
Preserved in radiant splendor
Like ancient ants caught in amber

This short poem represents a pause, a moment of reflection, about my journey. Its purpose is to look at the past while pondering the future. Reflection, a pause, a deep breath, are all for me, moments of renewal in the journey. They are a comfortable bench under a shady tree.

Reflecting on my life made me realize that my journey towards accepting my personal situation, taking responsibility to make it better, and offering service to others started very early in my life, with the example set by my parents, and was reinforced in my teens through the life-changing event of becoming a political refugee from Cuba. Both of my parents were highly educated, responsible individuals. My mother was a homemaker and a piano teacher. My father was a doctor of veterinary medicine, a business owner and a professor at the University of Havana in Cuba.

They instilled in their children the need to be responsible for your actions and the obligation to be kind to others. Noblesse oblige — the obligation to share one's special gifts or talents with others – was a concept discussed at our dinner table as a necessity in becoming a worthy human being. Another lesson often taught was to never lie, especially to yourself. My father would say, "I never wish things were better; I always make them better to the best of my ability. I never tell myself a lie; I want to know how bad things are, so I can accept them and fix them as soon as possible." My mom would say, "Your deeds will not be punished if you own up to them. There may be consequences for your actions, but you will never be punished for telling the truth about your mistakes." She was unfailingly true to her word and a harsh judge when told a lie.

When I was 15, political conditions in Cuba drove my brother and I into exile in the United States. This cataclysmic event essentially ended our childhood and rudely thrust us into manhood in the blink of an eye. During those years, my brother Eduardo and I lived in Camp Matecumbe, a refugee camp in the Florida Everglades. It was a Spanish version of *Lord of the Flies* – an experience best described as hellish, with overcrowding, poor living conditions and feelings of despair.

Many of my peers in the refugee camp wanted to think that the ordeal would soon pass and they would be sent back to Cuba. I instinctively knew better, even then. While at the library one day, I came across this quote from the Greek historian and general:

"The bravest are surely those who have the clearest vision
of what is before them, glory and danger alike,
and yet notwithstanding, go out to meet it."
—Thucydides

It was as though a bolt of lighting struck me and I knew I would never lie to myself about personal circumstances – ever – and would instead accept my situation and strive to make it better. I not only accepted my situation, but encouraged others at the camp to do the same. This attitude later served me well in college and corporate life, and continues to do so now in old age. Things are what they are and you must accept them without fear and strive to make them better.

As a young man, I was making my family's expectation of noblesse oblige mine in very personal terms. No matter what material things I possessed at any given time, I always possessed a sense of duty to others. My goal was to be fair and inclusive to others as I moved through life.

After earning a master's degree in human services — organizational development from Goddard College and a postgraduate executive certificate from Kelly School of Business of Indiana University in Bloomingdale, Indiana, I worked for a few years as a social worker and an administrator for a large nonprofit organization, the Evangelical Good Samaritan Society. Then I sought greener pastures and entered into a corporate career at Xerox Corp and later moved to the Eastman Kodak Company. To my amazement, I began to encounter success almost right from the start. During my 30-year corporate career at Xerox and Kodak, I was promoted 17 times, a fact that astounds me, surprises me and pleases me. During this time, one thing became clear: people saw me as ethical as I behaved in ways that were valued-centered, not just when convenient, but always. Others were concerned about their corporate success in a way that prompted them to compromise their values more readily. I had overcome the odds that were truly life and death, certainly at an emotional level and, while in Cuba, on a physical level, as well. The professional perils of corporate life, while threatening to others, became a game to me, much like chess.

My customers came to view me as an ally and a reliable partner. They told me I served them well by keeping their needs in mind, searching for the product or solution that benefited them before considering any profit motive. By gaining their trust, I gained their loyalty. Demonstrating my value of noblesse oblige was not only limited to my customers; I was there to help my employees, too. I helped inclusion of minorities in the workforces at both Xerox Corporation and the Eastman Kodak Company. This included members of minority groups as well as people who had been shunned because of their sexual orientation.

At Kodak, working in Worldwide Directorship for lean and customer satisfaction, I in collaboration with others — most notably my boss Steven Ramirez and colleague Cindy Clauss — brought me further success. I developed a customer-first model that required all employees to identify their customers by name and set forth plans of action that explained their actions toward their customers. Serving the customers first and right was at the heart of that model. That model became a guiding document and a way to bring life to our contractual obligations to any customer.

We launched the initiative worldwide and visited Europe, Latin America, and Canada together. The training and concept were translated into seven languages. Best of all we made friends in in every business unit; at every level; in every aspect of the organization; From Toronto, Canada, to Sao Paolo, Brazil, to Chalon, France and to Guadalajara, Mexico, we brought a message of doing well by doing good things for others-our customers. In all of my dealings with customers and employees, I chose to humanize people and promote common values as a foundation of trust and interdependence.

After retiring from the corporate world, I took a job teaching Psychology at Washington State University. Reflecting on my six years of teaching, I realized that my last big reward in the work world came from my students. In 2017, I was the recipient of the Chancellor's Medallion for Teaching Excellence at Washington State University. In presenting the award, the student body vice president and the chancellor each cited the unanimous vote of the Student Body Awards Committee in supporting my nomination for the award, as well as the narrative of the nomination, which centered around my involvement with and commitment to my students. One student said, "Brouwer will not let you give up on yourself — he listens, he counsels, he cajoles and he pushes until you do what you need to succeed." Bringing the best out in others by sharing my knowledge and experiences has been and continues to be my way of serving them. This quality stems from the values taught by my parents right from childhood — noblesse oblige.

By reflecting on my life at the onset of my retirement, I realized that I did not need to reinvent myself in my golden years, because I realized that what has truly always made me happy is to be of service to others; that I have donated my life to others. I am not a saint nor a selfless person; I do watch out for my own wellbeing and health. Things seldom make me happy, but people do. In that sense, meaningful aging for me has become the perfecting of what has worked well for me — an affirmation of my desire to be happy by being with others and doing for others.

As I continue my journey in the later phase of life, I have observed that taking responsibility, engaging in lifelong learning and serving others over time has become a habit and a set of skills for living for me. This has also made me humble and allows me to become purposeful about my own daily existence by proactively choosing what I do to impact others in a positive way. I look for opportunities to do things for the family, friends and strangers alike. I am never happier than when doing errands or other tasks for my spouse, children or grandchildren, or giving a helping hand to a friend or a former student who need assistance, or proactively engaging with strangers to identify ways I can help meet their needs. To ensure that I remain humble at all times and in all situations, I review my mission statement every day – create harmony at home, achieve excellence in work and provide service to others –as a way of ensuring that I am focused on living my life with purpose and meaning. Without humility, you have no desire to assess yourself for serving others.

> "Humility is not thinking less of yourself,
> it's thinking of yourself less."
> — C.S. Lewis

This quote from C.S. Lewis, a noted British writer and theologist, remind us that thinking of yourself less is indeed a good and freeing thing. It allows you to focus on the important things in life, which in the end benefits you. The act of giving and investing in people and ideas other than yourself becomes an affirming life experience. My observation over time is that people who have chosen to be externally focused on the good of others are happy and emotionally healthy people. Their wellbeing is a consequence of their conduct and it's an inducement to further positive behavior. Focusing outside of yourself is, in fact, essential for a healthy inner world.

My other observation in retirement is that people who stay positive as they age are not cynical. If you are a cynic, you find less good in others and tend to become isolated. Trusting may at times result in being emotionally hurt; but even then, you can learn and remain positive and open to the learning experience. Not being cynical keeps you open to opportunities, surprises and the goodness of others. Being cynical essentially forecloses those options. Cynical people end their days telling others, "I told you so," and they tend to exist in a state of anxiety and anger.

This journey of aging is not a linear or tidy proposition. There are negative aspects associated with growing old, such as physical limitations caused by the process of aging. I was a track and field standout in high school and college, and I have always enjoyed being physically active. While I can no longer run a record-setting sprint in the quarter-mile, I still walk approximately three miles each day, and far more than that on most days. I also do resistance training at the gym three days a week. Both activities are not only good for my body, but for my mind, too. Staying active is also consistent with my personal mission statement in that the walking I do is to serve myself and my dog by keeping us healthy, and I go to the gym with my wife since exercising together helps keep us in harmony as a couple.

This process of self betterment and continuous learning makes the quality of life in aging not only possible but fun. Celebration of the moment happens when you learn, the joy of aha moments, ensured by your own efforts. It also provides a sense of control over your daily existence that keeps you focused on the process of living a productive life. This becomes important in particular when you become aware of the fact that you have fewer tomorrows than you have yesterdays. Length of life is a gift, quality of life is an investment.

My friend Baldev explains that people have different mindsets towards aging, whether a fixed mindset or dynamic mindset. Even the most casual perusal of this model reveals the personal benefits and affirming qualities of the dynamic mindset. As I write this, I am in my early 70s, while Baldev is a few years older than I. Not once in our correspondence or conversations have we ever talked about anything other than the future, including exciting ideas for the years to come. This outlook is a consequence of having a dynamic mindset that propels you into the future and keeps your mind and body committed to the business of living life in the moment, life as an active manifestation of what is good and worthy within us, and life as a journey of discovery. My body and sometimes my mind may not be as potent as they were when I was a young man, however my spirit is many times stronger and, in many ways, far more capable and optimistic than at any period over the past seven decades.

The dynamic mindset is not a frenetic, headlong race towards a false and naïve denial of inevitable death. It is not a vapid "whoever dies with the most toys wins" view of life. It is a celebration of life through assertive personal actions, continuous improvement and unrelenting personal responsibility. This results in periods of reflection, a celebration, and an affirmation of life at its best.

The gains attained by following the dynamic mindset in our advanced years are consequential and significant. Baldev rewarded me by the kind invitation to participate and contribute to this, his current book. He offered me no material thing. He simply invited me to play with him – two old men at play; two people playing with ideas about the future; two friends measuring the last milestone not in fear of death, but in raucous celebration of life.

Aging Quality is a Choice

By sharing his story and demonstrating his dynamic mindset built upon beliefs of personal responsibility, ceaseless learning, a better life and service to others, Enrique reminds us that although we cannot stop aging, we can choose how to age. In other words, the quality of our golden years highly depends upon our choices. Enrique's following two assertions can greatly help seniors make the right choice when it comes to living a quality life and enjoying the last phase of their lives.

Length of life is a gift; quality of life is an investment: This statement says it all. Life is a precious gift and what we make of this gift depends upon how much we choose to invest in it to make it meaningful. This is true for every phase of human life, including our advanced years. Most seniors succumb to the classic belief that fate determines the quality of our lives in our remaining years; as such, we should just accept whatever comes our way and not expend any effort to improve the outcome. On the contrary, Enrique reminds us that it is our responsibility to shape the quality of our life with these words: "taking responsibility, engaging in lifelong learning and serving others over time has become a habit and a set of skills for living for me. This has also made me humble and allows me to become purposeful about my own daily existence by proactively choosing to impact others in a positive way. To ensure that I remain humble at all times and in all situations, I review my mission statement every day – *create harmony at home, achieve excellence in work and provide service to others* –as a way of safeguarding that I am focused on living my life with purpose and meaning.

Reflection, a pause, a deep breath, are all moments of renewal in the journey: Seniors who understand that it is within their power to choose how to shape the quality of life in the last phase still face a dilemma: Their predicament is what to pursue for a meaningful and joyful life in the golden years. In other words, they worry about what their next mission should be. Sadly, many start listening to and watching other seniors who are seemingly happy and decide to blindly follow some of them without reflecting on their own lives. However, their resultant short-term gratification quickly turns into confusion and frustration. After careful reflection on his experiences and learnings from his life, Enrique concluded: "*Meaningful aging for me has become the perfecting of what has worked well for me – an affirmation of my desire to be happy by being with others and doing for others.*"

Without reflecting on his past life, Enrique, like many other seniors, might have blindly followed someone else, made a revision of his cherished life mission and spent the balance of his golden years chasing someone else's goals only to find out too late that he was in pursuit of a mirage. Seniors can do themselves a great favor by taking this lesson: *The secret to finding the right mission for living in your golden years can be* found largely in the life you've already lived, divulged by a serious contemplation of the events and learning of your past.

"We do not learn from experience.
We learn from reflecting on experience."
—John Dewey, American Philosopher

Throughout his life, Enrique realized success and happiness through the power of his dynamic mindset, built on his beliefs of personal responsibility, ceaseless learning, pursuing a better life and service to others. It was the power of that dynamic mindset which transformed the frightening vision of a refugee boy into a life of esteemed respect from his colleagues, customers, and students; and abundant love from his family.

1960   2008

What a transition!

There is a bigger question here! What was that catalyst which enabled Enrique to keep his dynamic mindset intact in both periods of adversity and unprecedented success in his long life?

In my humble opinion, that catalyst was—not discarding his family value of *noblesse oblige*—*the obligation to share one's special gifts or talents with others.* That value was vividly evident throughout his life— encouraging his co-residents in the refugee camp to accept the brutal fact of their exile and taking responsibility to make their situation better; sharing his meagre materialistic resources with others during his college, helping customers and employees in his professional career at Xerox Corporation and the Eastman Kodak Co.; helping students to become the best while teaching at Washington State University; and more importantly, making the golden years of his life meaningful by offering his services to help all around him at all times and in all situations. Indeed, his dynamic mindset was further reinforced by the power of that value.

"Noblesse oblige, or superior advantages, bind you to larger generosity."
—Ralph Waldo Emerson

Chapter 13

A Warrior Missionary

Vijaya Srinivasan

Long-term and Subacute Care Regional Administrator

"The surgeon went over the entire lung transplant procedure and then he looked into my eyes and said, 'There is no guarantee you will survive or thrive after receiving a transplant. Do you still want to go through with this?' I smiled at the doctor and asked, 'Do I have any other choice?' "

This is Vijaya Srinivasan, 68, a native of India and a retired long-term and subacute care administrator in the United States, describing her second encounter with death. What made this remarkable woman stared death in the eye twice enabling her to witness the glorious wedding of her daughter and spend quality time with her grandson Kailash? Let us find that secret in her life story, told here, in her own words:

Facing Death

by *Vijaya Srinivasan*

I come from a family of freedom fighters and I often draw upon the courage and bravery of my ancestors. Since moving to America in 1973, knowing no one but my husband, I have built a life here and established a successful career as an administrator for a licensed nursing and rehabilitation care center in New Jersey. I have never been one to shy away from challenges – whether I go after them, or life presents them to me. Death has stared me right in the face twice, and this has shaped my mindset to embrace whatever comes my way and not to fear it.

My first health scare occurred in 2003. During a trip to India, I got very sick on the flight to Chennai, my favorite city. I was bleeding heavily, so I went to a gynecologist in India and she told me I needed to get a biopsy done immediately. The gynecologist gave me some medication to help me temporarily and I had to shorten my trip and return to the United States. Once I returned, I had the biopsy and my doctor called me immediately afterwards and said I had endometrial cancer and needed a hysterectomy.

I went through the surgery and then had to consult a specialist for chemotherapy. I learned that since we caught the cancer at a very early stage, I did not need any chemotherapy treatment. We sought a second opinion and the specialist was amazed that we were able to recognize the symptoms at such an early stage; that it is very rare to receive a diagnosis so early. I realized how blessed I was, and my faith in God only strengthened, which proved important when I faced death for a second time.

In 2010, we made another trip to India, and when I returned, I had a really bad cough for six months. It steadily got worse and no medication would alleviate it. I saw a pulmonologist and was misdiagnosed with Farmers Lung.

As a lifelong plant lover, I was devastated when my doctor ordered me to get rid of all of my plants. Even after our home was plant-free, my cough still didn't go away. I was not only coughing, but also experiencing extreme shortness of breath and could not walk continuously for even a few minutes.

I was put on oxygen therapy at night and still was not getting better. After having a biopsy of my lungs, the doctors still weren't able to figure out what was wrong with me. I then needed extra oxygen 24/7, and I went to work with an oxygen tank, introducing the tank as "my buddy" that helps me breathe.

Vijaya Srinivasan working with her "buddy," a portable oxygen tank

My staff was visibly upset and sad because they did not like seeing me in this condition. I had to stay strong and pacify my staff's worries and ask them to be brave together with me, so that with our positive faith, I would get better while I carried out my work duties as usual.

Eventually, my doctor told me I had to stop working and I started going to pulmonary rehabilitation five days a week. Even though I was doing everything I could, my condition deteriorated and it was clear that if I wanted to survive, I had to receive a double lung transplant. My son helped me get admitted into the lung transplant program at the Hospital of the University of Pennsylvania in 2012, and there I met a very compassionate and skilled surgeon. The surgeon went over the entire lung transplant procedure and then he looked into my eyes and said, "There is no guarantee you will survive or thrive after receiving a transplant. Do you still want to go through with this?" I smiled at the doctor and asked, "Do I have any other choice?"

Once I was on the list to receive a double transplant my daughter and my best friend's daughter chanted 108 times *Hanuman Chalisa* as required by Hindu religion to praise and invoke Lord Hanuman, the Hindu God of Strength. I strongly believe that God only gives us what we can handle, so I was confident that I would persevere through this.

On October 17, 2012, at 4 a.m., we got a call to go to the Hospital of the University of Pennsylvania. The surgery took 10 ½ hours and, thankfully, everything went well. But while the surgeon said I got the best lungs possible, he also reminded me and my family of the risk factors associated with the surgery.

I was in the intensive care unit for two weeks after the transplant. I did not recognize anyone and could not speak. After two days, I slowly opened my eyes and was transferred to a recovery floor, where I continued to heal. It took a month before I was discharged from the hospital. I then had several setbacks and had to be readmitted to the hospital. Finally, I came home and started therapy three days a week for three months at the Hospital of the University of Pennsylvania. At the end of those three months, the transplant team did not feel I was recovering properly, so my therapy was extended for two more months. During this time, I faced a number of challenges and was barely sleeping because I was worried that if I moved while I was asleep I might dislocate my newly transplanted lungs.

MEANINGFUL AGING

My recovery was very, very slow and it took me one year to start walking normally and really recuperate. All along, my faith, my supportive family and my friends gave me strength. My positive attitude on life made a big impact, too. I never gave up and fought every step of the way to get my life back. I am so grateful that I now have a new lease on life. Thanks to my faith and strength from my strong belief in taking personal responsibility, I have been able to see my daughter get married and am now enjoying spending time with my beautiful grandson, Kailash.

I have learned that life is not easy; it is like a river on which you travel with lots of winding turns along the way. We are here to travel on that river, learn along the way and enjoy what we can. Life's challenges grow our spirits and bring us closer to the divine, and our suffering can even be a gift in helping us to focus on what truly is important. Life is a challenge, a pilgrimage, a journey, a mission. My personal mantra is: Life is about giving love and helping others, and wanting to make a difference in any way I can and having strong faith in God.

What does aging mean to me: To me, aging is about engaging in meaningful and purposeful living. As I age, I want to be conscious of how my inner and outer life is changing and meet those shifts with a positive attitude, embracing what comes. I am not attached to being young, and see my senior years as an opportunity to share the wisdom I've gathered. It's important for me to attend to my inner life through spirituality and my exterior life through service to others. I am not afraid of getting old. I believe that, as I age, I have begun to realize what truly matters and focus my energy there. For example, I now prioritize my health in a way I never did before because I always used to be concerned about taking care of others and pursuing my career. Now, I realize if I don't take care of myself, I won't be available for anyone else.

Beliefs shape my mindset of aging: For 40 years, I worked in the long-term care and rehabilitation services industry. I started as a bookkeeper and eventually received my license as a long-term and sub-acute care administrator. I then held a regional leadership position, in which I managed several long-term and subacute care rehabilitation facilities in New Jersey, Pennsylvania and Connecticut. Working closely with the elderly population has taught me that life is very short and it is important to do whatever you can to make a positive difference in the lives of others while you are here.

During my career, I have grown to understand the value of being a lifelong learner, which is also the secret to aging dynamically. I have also learned that my beliefs affect how I see myself and others, and I have made a commitment to having a positive mindset in terms of always looking for the good in others.

I have personally experienced how my parents made their golden years a rewarding time for them. While in his 80s, my dad began writing books and composing spiritual songs with my mother, and they worked together passionately on these projects and enjoyed every moment of their final years.

Continuous learning is very important to aging dynamically and, as I mentioned above, being a lifelong learner and meeting every day with curiosity and wonder is important. I know that I am creating my own happiness and seizing every opportunity that comes my way to learn are important factors in leading a joyful life. For example, when I was 50 years old, my husband and I began taking music classes together and this brought us lots of joy. We also started to practice yoga while in our mid-50s.

When I was 62, we moved to a retirement community in Florida. There, I took a leadership role in creating opportunities for members of the community to learn continuously. I started a music group that met weekly to practice and perform in many celebrations. I helped to organize a Ladies Club, through which women could explore ways to improve our lives. We also organized several different activities, such as yoga, arts and crafts, dance, card games, etc., which made us engage the use of both our bodies and our minds. The ladies in this group look forward to the weekly meetings, during which we learn from and with our peers.

Personal responsibility is really critical when aging, because you alone are totally responsible for your life. This is a fundamental life principle for me, and I cannot blame anyone or make excuses if I do not accomplish my goals. During my entire adult life, I have struggled with weight management and my overall health because I had prioritized my career and family over my own well-being. When my brother visited me after a long period of being apart, he was very upset that I had not been taking care of myself at all. He helped me see that I had neglected myself and that my poor health could result in me becoming a burden to my family. He made me think about how I had created this problem, what I could do differently, and how I could improve my health by taking the right actions. After reflecting on this, I made a plan to finally take responsibility for my health. I hired a coach and personal trainer to help me improve my eating habits and encourage me to exercise daily. I also changed my family's diet and began cooking healthy food. Through this experience, I learned that I am ultimately in charge of my life.

Aligning passion with purpose is important when it comes to giving your life deeper meaning: For me, feeling purposeful is all about being of service to others and making their lives better. My Dad always said that, when you wake up in the morning, you need to feel that you are fulfilling a purpose. All my life, until I retired, I felt purposeful when waking up in the morning. While I was working, I was so busy I couldn't really think about creating meaning in my life; I just had to focus on getting things done. But now that I'm retired, I seek to intentionally create more meaning in my life. My Mom taught me to be compassionate and generous, so I live my life based on these values, which ultimately gives my life greater meaning. I relentlessly pursue my passion of providing service and making a difference in the lives of others.

When I found out my daughter was expecting her first child, I wanted to do whatever I could to help her so she could manage her career and family. I remembered what it was like when I was in that situation; I was very fortunate that my mom was able to help me, so I could continue to advance in my career. I asked my husband to consider moving to California so we could help our daughter. It was a big decision, but my husband and I moved to California, where we rented an apartment down the street from my daughter and took care for our grandson daily for eighteen months. We both felt very happy and joyful to be part of our grandson's life. Our lives were fulfilling and we immensely enjoyed our time with our grandson. His smiles made our day. The joy we experienced was unlike any joy we've had before. It was remarkable. Now we are back in our condo in the retirement community in Florida and wake up every day to make a positive difference in the lives of other residents here.

A True Legacy

"Why are you so insistent about going back to Florida in August — the peak month of the scorching summer?" I recently asked my wife.

"I miss the Ladies Club meetings!" she exclaimed..

"What? Just for that weekly meeting, you want us to torture ourselves in that heat?" I inquired, hoping she would change her mind.

"You will not understand, but I want to go," she replied.

As usual, I yielded to her request, but I also was curious as to why that weekly meeting meant so much to her. My perception of the Ladies Club was that it was merely an opportunity for the women to meet once a week to chit chat and socialize.

When we arrived at our condo in the Shantiniketan Retirement Community near Orlando on a Sunday afternoon that summer, we made a shocking discovery: only 35 families were home at the time. In fact, one of the organizers of the Ladies Club — Vijaya Srinivasan — had gone to California to help her daughter, who was expecting her first child. My wife sensed my anger over what appeared to be a futile trip. Before my anger exploded, she rushed to the club house to inquire if there were other activities taking place. Lo and behold, there were very few group activities in the summer, except the Ladies Club meeting every Monday. Relieved and anxious to quell my anger, she came back to our condo and proudly declared that the Ladies Club meeting would be the next day, as scheduled on Monday.

Given that most other activities had been cancelled for the summer, I was somewhat surprised to learn the Ladies Club was still meeting.

During the winter months, from January through March, when most families are residing in Florida, the retirement community bustles with physical, intellectual and spiritual activities, as well as various group discussions designed to uplift individual and community life. The Ladies Club meeting is among those group activities, taking place every Monday from 4 to 5 p.m. Amazingly, the Ladies Club is one of the activities that continues throughout the year. Rain or shine, winter or summer, any women who are present on any given Monday in the community, will without exception attend that meeting.

Ladies Club Meeting in Shantiiketan 2

Why is the Ladies Club meeting such an outlier, as compared with other programs and activities in this community?

Do the Ladies Club meetings offer women, their only chance to voice themselves in this male-dominated community, or does it provide a comfort zone in which they can express their fears and vulnerabilities when facing the challenges of old age? The answer to this question is none of the above. Rather, their commitment is a testament to the esteem and love they feel towards the founders of the group.

Even in their absence, the attendees feel their spirits guiding and encouraging them to be self-sufficient, proactive in decision-making and benevolent towards their fellow beings.

Just reading Vijaya Srinivasan's narrative about her triumphs and tribulations made me feel the remarkable power of her dynamic mindset, based on her strongly held beliefs of taking personal responsibility for what happens in her life; accepting life as a continuous adventure; embracing lifelong learning for becoming a better person; and, most important, transforming her passion for being compassionate to others into her commitment to the Ladies' Group and other similar activities.

Vijaya. Srinivasan's passion for serving others is not limited to organizing the Ladies Club, alone; it spans into many other areas through which she can make a positive difference for others. Along with the Ladies Club, she also started a glee club that also met weekly to practice and perform in many celebrations. She also took a leadership role in organizing several different activities such as yoga, arts and crafts, dance and card games designed to engage both the bodies and minds of seniors living in our community.

Her passion for serving others is not limited to just helping her peers. She's ready to spring into any situation in which she can lend a helping hand. This is evident from her statement: "I relentlessly pursue my passion of providing service and making a difference in the lives of others."

Armed with the powers of her dynamic mindset, Vijaya Srinivasan is defying the conventional wisdom of creating human legacy. Unlike the common belief that leaving a legacy has to be gigantic and is for the rich and famous, her life gives credence to these words of Robb Lucy, author of the book, Legacies are Not for Dead People, who wrote: "My legacy is something I create that connects and enhances lives now, and will continue to positively affect others when I am gone." Helping to establish a simple activity like the ladies club meetings is a great legacy as it is connecting people, enhancing their lives, and is continuing even when one or both of the founders aren't there.

With the zeal of a warrior and the compassion of a missionary, this remarkable lady has – and is – facing her life challenges with the utmost courage and faith, and she is making a positive difference in the lives of many. In addition to validating and living with the five key elements of a dynamic mindset about aging, Vijaya has become a role model for many and propagates the following truths:

1. *It is within our power to create and cement our legacy during our lifetime. By doing so, we not only make our human existence worthwhile, but also generate authentic happiness for ourselves in the process.*

2. *Authentic happiness generated through the process of creating and cementing our legacy in our advanced years makes our sufferings seem trivial and our contentment infinite.*

"If you are going to live, leave a legacy. Make a mark on the world that can't be erased."
—Maya Angelou

Chapter 14

A Habitual Novice

Dr. Thomas Mathew, MD

Founder and owner of Belize Spice Farm & Botanical Gardens

Southern Highway, Hellgate, Belize, Central America

"I will take a pass."

Despite the repeated requests of my wife and close friends to accompany them on an excursion from our cruise ship to the Spice Farm & the Botanical Gardens in Belize, I was in no mood to waste the afternoon by taking a trip to learn about spices I already use and look at plants I've probably seen before. There was no novelty there, I thought, preferring to read a book while lounging peacefully on the top deck of our ship, the Norwegian Pearl. Little did I know, when I eventually yielded to my wife's persuasive insistence to join the excursion, that it would lead me to meet Dr. Thomas Mathew, a self-described habitual learner, who I later would write about in this book about meaningful aging.

It was December of 2018 and 50 seniors from our retirement community in Florida were on a two-week cruise to the Panama Canal and seven ports in nearby countries: the Cayman Islands, Jamaica, Colombia, Guatemala, Costa Rica, Belize and Costa Maya, Mexico. For safety concerns in that region, we decided to only take excursions to the tourist places recommended and managed by the Norwegian Cruise Line, and the trip to the Belize Spice Farm & Botanical Gardens was among them.

Situated on the eastern coast of Central America, the small country of Belize is nestled between the shoreline of the Emerald Caribbean Sea and dense jungles. With its ancient Mayan ruins and popular scuba diving sites, including the Blue Hole and the second-largest barrier reef in the world, Belize is constantly featured in prestigious magazines such as *National Geographic* and it has become a favorite tourist destination. One of the most popular tours in the country is a visit to Belize Spice Farm & Botanical Gardens. Located in the largely rural Toledo District of Southern Belize, this is an enclave of more than 500 acres where you can explore an amazing array of orchards and spice and flower gardens.

During the hour-long bus ride from our ship to the farm, I was still lamenting the time I could have spent on the ship with my book. But as soon as we disembarked from the bus and entered the Spice Farm & Botanical Gardens, my aversion to the forced adventure started to melt away. The sweet smell of fresh flowers and aromatic spices infused me with a sense of pleasure and excitement.

For the next two and a half hours, we had a guided tour that included a trolley ride and walking through the grounds. It is the only place in the country that grows spices, in addition to rare, exotic trees such as mahogany, teak and rosewood. We also saw a huge variety of tropical and exotic fruits grown in the orchards, where we inhaled aromas and flavors of Surinam cherry, lychee, star apple, avocado, tropical blackberry and tamarind. A variety of pungent spices, including cumin, coriander, mustard seeds, ginger, turmeric, cinnamon and spicy red chili peppers, were grown there. Talking to some of the people working on the farm, I got the feeling they were quite excited and happy to be there. In the midst of our tour, we saw Cinnamon Hall—a dream venue for wedding celebrations, flanked by flowering arches that serve as the perfect backdrop for wedding pictures.

By the end of our tour, I was thankful that I had participated in the excursion and thanked my wife and friends for convincing me to come along. At the same time, I was curious about the person who had created this oasis. The tour guide informed us that the founder and owner was Dr. Thomas Mathew, a native of India who was an anesthesiologist in West Virginia before moving here more than 30 years ago to open the spice farm and gardens. Over time, he imported spice plants and other seedlings from his native India, introducing these to this region.

Any medical doctor sacrificing the comfortable life of the United States and settling in a little country like Belize, and farming spices and flowers will naturally raise curiosity. Members of my group, many of whom also were from India or had other connections there, were curious to meet Dr. Mathew, so our tour guide arranged for us to meet with him.

After exchanging the classic respectful Indian greeting of *Namaste*, Dr. Mathew introduced himself to our group and expressed his thanks for our visit to his farm. In response to our inquiries about how he landed here, he explained that he and his wife, Tessy, had flown to Belize to go scuba diving years before and fell in love with the country. So they settled here 30 years ago and started the *Spice Farm & Botanical* Gardens there. With help from the Belizean government, they imported seeds and cuttings of spice plants, exotic fruit trees, teak and mahogany trees, ornamental plants and more to create the Belize Spice Farm and Botanical Gardens.

Dr. Thomas Mathew (second from right)
and author Baldev Seekri (fourth from right)

That was nothing less than a fairy tale—a medical doctor, flying a plane, to scuba dive, in a remote country, and starting a plantation of spices and other exotic trees and flower gardens seemed fiction at first, but it was a stark reality as we were seeing that man in real flesh smiling and relishing every word he was speaking!

In addition to admiring the risks he took to pursue his dreams, I also was impressed by his energy and enthusiasm – the same delightful energy and enthusiasm I felt from his employees who worked on the farm.

I wanted to learn more about what sparked his spirit, especially in this later phase of his life, but, alas, the tour bus driver announced that it was time for our group to head back to the ship. As we were leaving, I told Dr. Mathew that I was writing a book about meaningful aging and asked if he would be willing to share the story of his life and his views on aging. To my delight, he agreed. Here is Dr. Mathew's story, in his own words.

MY JOURNEY

By Dr. Thomas Mathew, MD

Staying busy has become a habit for me. Working as an anesthesiologist in the operating room of a hospital in a small town in West Virginia nurtured this habit. But spending my entire working life in an operating room did not appeal to me. I was afraid I would miss out on many of the things I had dreamed of as a child, including one day owning a farm. I also was very much aware that I would not be able to continue working as an anesthesiologist when I get older. But going back to India to pursue my dream of farming seemed difficult due to distance, government regulations and the possibility of family interference.

So after becoming an anesthesiologist, I secured a job at a hospital in a small town in West Virginia and settled there. In my spare time, I focused my attention on expanding my hobbies and learning other activities. Photography was a hobby I had started as a teenager. By subscribing to magazines and reading books, I gained enough knowledge to create a lab where I developed large color prints. My children were my models and, very soon, large photographs replaced wallpaper in one of the rooms of my home. With digital photography, it has become easier to produce these types of prints, but I still try to be creative using the digital tools available.

Learning new things has been important to me since my childhood, thanks to my parents and grandparents, who taught all of their children the value of learning and pursuing higher education. The challenge of learning new and different things has always inspired me, so when the challenge and the excitement of photography started to wane, I took advantage of night classes offered by a local vocational school for adults. Courses in carpentry, electrical wiring and air conditioning helped me develop skills that are still useful to me today. I have also attempted to learn welding, small engine repair, and computer repair, as well as elementary auto mechanic classes. Each one of these specialty courses has given me a glimpse into different worlds.

Flying and scuba diving were two other hobbies I pursued for many years, when I could find the time. After I acquired enough flying experience and was instrument rated, I flew with my wife to several airports in California, including the Brown Field Municipal Airport in San Diego, John Wayne Airport in Orange County and the Catalina Airport in Avalon — all before GPS was available.

In addition, scuba diving trips took me to many Caribbean islands. One of my favorite scuba diving magazines, *Skin Diver,* had an issue focusing on Belize. I kept that issue and finally made it to Belize for a diving vacation in 1988. My wife and I rented a vehicle and hired an aircraft to see as much of this beautiful country as possible. Seeing the tropical land and the beautiful gardens there reignited my interest in starting a farm and Belize seemed ideal for this endeavor. I made several trips to southern Belize, where I thought the soil was fertile, based on what I had seen looking at the trees in the jungle. So I finally decided to jump in and pursue my dream of creating and owning my own farm.

We made a decision to settle in the southern part of Belize and started the Golden Stream Plantation in the Toledo District of Belize in 1990, where we grew cacao and citrus trees. Over time, the farm grew to include various spice plants, exotic fruit trees and teak and mahogany trees, as well as a large array of ornamental flowers. After 30 years of growth and few setbacks, we finally have a citrus grove and the biggest vanilla and spice farm in the region, as well as a thriving business in agrotourism.

Tessy and Thomas Mathew

The Golden Stream Village was a very small community in 1989. Many members of the community worked for me, and they helped me as much as I helped them. However, there was quite a suspicion and misunderstanding in the beginning. Maya Indians have many reasons to be suspicious of outsiders, and we were outsiders when we began our farm. We now have about 50 skilled and unskilled staff members from three neighboring villages. I believe they are happy and proud to work for my farm – and it shows.

"Is this what I wanted? Maybe. One never knows where your crazy life takes you!"

In his initial write-up, Dr. Mathew gave me plenty of information about his motivation to settle in Belize and start the spice and botanical farm. However, he failed to explain his thought process when it came to developing and nurturing a mindset that empowered him to find joy at this stage of his life, without regard to his advanced age or fear of the uncertainties of the future. His short write-up failed to capture the jubilation, humility and the enthusiasm he displayed in just a few minutes of interaction with those of us involved in the excursion to his farm. I wanted to know what shaped his adventurous mindset — his beliefs and philosophy about life, particularly in his senior years.

So I sent him excerpts from this book that compare the classic and dynamic mindsets of aging, explaining the various constituents of these two contrasting frames of mind. I asked Dr. Mathew to digest that information in light of his philosophy towards life and the choices he has made. In that reflection, I asked him to determine which constituents of the classic or dynamic mindset played a major role in his thinking and choices. I am very grateful to Dr. Mathew, who explained his mindset in the following summary:

My Mindset about Life and Aging

By Dr. Thomas Mathew, MD

I consider aging part of a natural process. Accepting aging and owning your age — which includes making necessary changes and setting realistic goals — makes aging more meaningful and enjoyable. Reflecting on the choices made and how they turned out can invoke different emotions, negative and positive, and leads to the question of: What if? The key is not to get bogged down in the what ifs and instead remember that the possibilities are infinite. Knowing that life is a journey that will end one day and that we will leave our engagements does not make me sad, but rather inspires me to enjoy my journey and do some good along the way.

Our mindset as we age must be dynamic. We are the product of our genes, our environments and our experiences in life. While we cannot change our genetic makeup, our environments and experiences are constantly changing. As such, I am a different person with every fleeting moment of time. Accordingly, my mindset must be dynamic to embrace the new realities of my life at any given time and be prepared to grasp the opportunities and tackle the obstacles presented. Without this dynamic mindset, I never would have had the courage to take risks, such as settling in Belize and starting a new life here. Having a dynamic mindset is even more important as we age. In the absence of the dynamic mindset, we tend to give up in the face of our limitations and sufferings and focus on our fate rather than on our efforts to make our existence more manageable and meaningful. This may be one of the main reasons that I don't worry much about the future and tend to focus on the moment —every day, I am living my life and grasping the opportunities presented.

Beliefs can limit as well as uplift you. Beliefs developed through lifelong loyalty to family, religion, race and country can be limiting when it comes to realizing your full potential, however, they also can protect you from harm and may help unleash your potential. The key is to periodically check the validity of these beliefs against our changing realities and make changes if necessary. Periodic examination of our beliefs brings us closer to the realities of where we are at any given time in our lives. If our beliefs prove to be outdated, we can discard them; on the contrary, if they are proven to be correct, we can move on with those stronger beliefs and a higher level of confidence.

Continual Learning is indeed the soul of meaningful life. I am living proof of this reality. As explained earlier, keeping busy is a habit for me and the thing that has helped me the most is to develop and nurture this habit through constant learning. In one way, I am a habitual novice, always learning something new. As photography became less challenging, I ventured into learning other crafts, such as carpentry, welding, small engine repair and other trades. As the medical profession became monotonous, I looked for other things that would continue to challenge me and make me learn, so I ventured into farming. Even now, 30 years after starting the spice farm, not a day passes when I am not experimenting making something grow better or improving the appearance of the Spice Farm & the Botanical Gardens to make it more aesthetic. This spirit of adventure and experimentation is clearly contagious, given that the 50 or so associates working on the farm are always very excited to try new things. They learn from me and I learn from them.

Downsizing our materialistic lifestyle is beneficial. Trimming our materialistic attachments in old age and, eventually, in retirement, gives you the freedom to experiment with your creativity and face failures/success/enjoyment with a willingness to change your plans and goals. This is essential to attaining your somewhat elusive or non-definable goals in your old age. Materialistic things that are symbols of status and power in our middle age become unnecessary baggage as we travel through our advanced years. They breed the feeling that we need to be better than others, rather than pursuing what is most meaningful to us to give us genuine happiness. With our simple life on the farm, my wife Tessy and I feel liberated from the burden of acquiring materialistic belongings which frees us to make our lives – and those around us – more enjoyable.

Pursuing my passion is essential for a larger purpose. My life has taught me that in the absence of a passion or passions, our life is comatose and our existence is meaningless and robotic. Pursuing our passions generates a sort of gratification and/or satisfaction that adds zest to our daily functioning. If we also make our pursuit of passion a means for creating a positive difference in the lives of others, we experience phenomenal happiness and ceaseless energy to continue in this pursuit.

This is the precious lesson I have learned through pursuing my passion of farming here at the spice farm. My pursuit of my passion for farming has created jobs that enable more than 50 local residents to earn a living from an exciting line of work, assist the local economy and provide a state-of-the-art tourist attraction for the country of Belize. Is this purpose aligned with my passion — the reason for my longevity and happiness? Perhaps!

In conclusion, as long as my mindset remains dynamic and keeps me motivated to take responsibility for my personal situation, to learn every day and to shape a better quality of life for myself, my wife and all the people who work for me on the farm, I will not have the time to worry about any additional wrinkle, any additional year added to my age or any additional challenge to my existence, and the journey of my life will continue unabated to create joy and meaning. "

Aging Journey Enriched

"It is good to have an end to journey toward;
but it is the journey that matters in the end."
—Ernest Hemingway

Dr. Thomas Mathew's life is not only an interesting story of adventure and learning, but it is also a great lesson for all of us, especially seniors who worry about the end of life rather than focusing on making the last phase of their life journey meaningful and joyful.

Throughout his life, Dr. Mathew aspired for novel challenges and enriched his life journey by pursuing his passions and making a positive difference in the lives of others.

Dr. Thomas Mathew (left) farming in 1994 at the spice farm

The more I learn about Dr. Mathew's joyful life, the more clearly I can see the power of his dynamic mindset steering his life journey. His belief in the transience of life and his perception of aging as a natural process — a journey to undertake without constant worry — is clearly reflected in his these sentiments: *Knowing that life is a journey that will end one day and that we will leave our engagements here does not make me sad, but rather inspires me to enjoy my journey and do some good along the way.*

Dr. Mathew's belief in the importance of continual learning was forged early on with the values instilled by his parents during his childhood. That belief was further tempered by his life experiences, transforming him into what he describes as a habitual novice — exploring and learning new things and making them meaningful for himself and for others. That belief is also evident in another of his comments: *Even now, 30 years after starting the spice farm, not a day pass when I am not experimenting making something grow better or improving the appearance of the Spice Farm &Botanical Gardens to make it more aesthetic.*

Another great lesson seniors can learn from Dr. Mathew's life is how to sculpt or shape a better quality of our aging journey by lightening our belongings. As he notes: *Trimming our materialistic attachments in old age and, eventually, retirement gives you the freedom to experiment with your creativity and face failures/success/enjoyment with a willingness to change your plans and goals. This is essential to attaining your somewhat elusive or non-definable goals in your old age.*

Finally, the ultimate vitality and criticality of a dynamic mindset of aging is summarized brilliantly by Dr. Mathew in these few words: *In the absence of the dynamic mindset, we tend to give up in the face of our limitations and sufferings and start believing in our fate rather than in our efforts to make our existence meaningful. This may be one of the main reasons that I don't worry much about the future and tend to focus on the very day I am living my life.*

All of us who are seniors already undertaking the journey of aging in the last phase of our lives, as well those who will be starting their journey soon after retirement, can learn from Dr. Thomas Mathew's life story to embrace the power of a dynamic mindset to enrich their own journey of aging.

"When setting out on a journey, do not seek advice from those who never left home."
—Rumi, Sufi mystic and poet

Section 3

Developing Your Dynamic Mindset

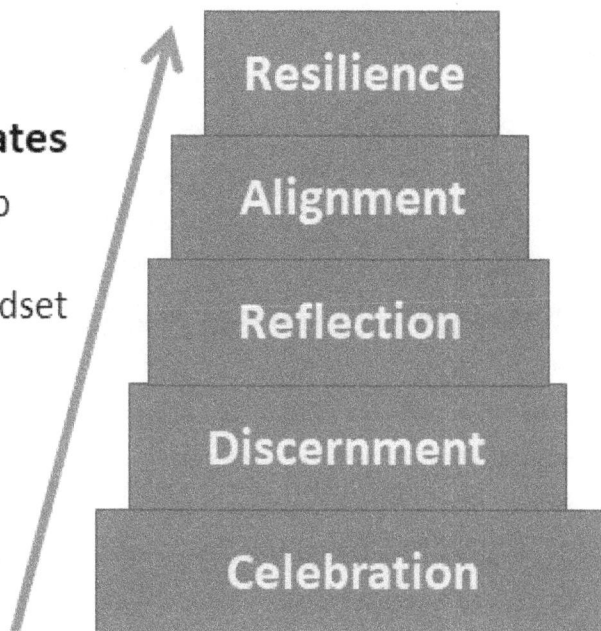

5 Mandates
to Develop
A
Dynamic Mindset
of
Aging

Resilience

Alignment

Reflection

Discernment

Celebration

Baldev K Seekri

Learning is a treasure that will follow its owner everywhere.
— Chinese Proverb

This book has introduced you to 10 remarkable senior citizens who not only embody the spirit of meaningful aging, but also demonstrate the five elements of the archetypal dynamic mindset, which I introduced back in Chapter 3.

As you may recall, the dynamic mindset is based on acknowledging the realities of aging, while also realizing the need to change your mindset to focus on the things that are most important to you to bring you genuine fulfillment in the final states of life.

These 10 seniors have certainly done that!

Dr. Paul James Maryan, retired Air Marshal S. Raghavendran, Vishwakant Mankodi, Mai Donohue and Dolores Cummins shared inspiring episodes of their personal lives that brought to life the essentials of the dynamic mindset of aging. Carol Young, Dr. Dinesh Shah, Enrique Brouwer, Vijaya Srinivasan and Dr. Thomas Mathews also shared their personal journeys, demonstrating how they have assimilated most, if not all, of the elements of the dynamic mindset of aging and have found meaning and joy in the last chapter of their lives as a result.

In addition, these 10 extraordinary people offer valuable insights the rest of us can use to keep our own dynamic mindset of aging strong and healthy as we journey through our advanced years. Drawing from their wisdom, coupled with the insight of experts and my personal experience during 15 years of retirement, I have created these five essential mandates to help you develop, refresh and reinforce your own dynamic mindset of aging. These mandates will help you continue your journey of aging with positive anticipation and contentment. I have presented these in a sequential manner, with each step providing an essential piece of wisdom intended to help you master the intricacies of the next step.

1.) **CELEBRATION:** This is the foundation upon which you will build your dynamic mindset of meaningful aging. You need to learn that your uniqueness is embedded in your talents (your natural abilities), which are manifested through your strengths. By learning to identify your strengths and reinforcing them with unwavering commitment to constantly use and nurture them, you can identify those qualities that make you unique. With strong and genuine strengths, you will have a clear and uplifting view of your uniqueness. In the next chapter on celebration, you will learn to recognize your strengths, remove barriers that may prevent you from further developing

192

them and identify strategies to celebrate your strengths and other qualities that contribute to your uniqueness.

2.) DISCERNMENT: After recognizing and celebrating your uniqueness, the next step is to understand precisely what aging is all about, how mindset is formed and why it is important to adopt a dynamic mindset for meaningful aging. This discernment is essential to help shield you from the myths and misinformation about aging that are rampant in society. In the ensuing chapter on discernment, you will learn how to distinguish among opinions, facts and truths to establish an objective mindset towards aging.

3.) REFLECTION: After acknowledging your uniqueness and strengths and gaining confidence by discerning the truth about aging, you are now ready to take the next step: to reflect upon the sources of your personal gratification and intuitive happiness. You will identify these sources through deep personal reflection about your passions and the purpose of your life. In the upcoming chapter on reflection, you will learn the difference between focusing and reflecting on these issues; the process involved in self-reflection; and the importance of making self-reflection a regular habit. You also will learn how to use these tools to pinpoint the activities and actions that generate gratification and genuine happiness in your life. Although continual self-reflection is a necessity in every phase of human life, it is of paramount importance in your senior years in order to determine and adjust the direction of your life journey based on the quickly changing realities that occur in our advanced years.

4.) ALIGNMENT: Using the first three steps to identify your strengths, discern the importance of mindset and reflect on those things that bring you personal satisfaction, you're now ready for the fourth step: aligning your passions with the larger purpose of helping and serving others. Dr. Gene D. Cohen, a psychiatrist who pioneered research into geriatric mental health, tells us that human creativity is the highest in the second half of life. In the ensuing chapter on alignment, you will learn more about the essential ingredients of alignment by combining reflection and creativity to identify a way to tailor your passions towards service to others. This alignment is essential to solidify your dynamic mindset of aging in the midst of the changing realities of your senior years.

5.) **RESILIENCE:** The last but not least essential mandate to develop and reinforce your dynamic mindset of aging is to learn resilience. Resilience is critical in order to face, prevent, endure and/or recover from a multitude of physical and mental adversities that you are likely to face at some point in your advanced years. In the subsequent chapter on resilience, you will learn the physical, cognitive, emotional and spiritual domains of resilience and how to remove potential barriers to developing resilience. You will also learn why developing a positive dynamic mindset is vital to resilience. In addition, we will examine how individual resilience becomes intertwined with community resilience, especially for the increasing number of seniors choosing to live in retirement communities. We also will examine how and why the inhabitants of some retirement communities tend to live longer and happier lives.

These five mandates for developing a dynamic mindset of aging need to become your mantra, commandment, directive or whatever you choose to call it in your journey towards meaningful aging. Understanding the importance of these mandates and dedicating yourself to pursuing them genuinely – at all times and in all situations – will greatly improve the quality of your dynamic mindset and lead to a higher level of contentment in your remaining years.

Chapter 15

Celebration

The more you praise and celebrate your life,

the more there is in life to celebrate.

—Oprah Winfrey

Contrary to the conventional practice of celebrating after a task is completed and the goal is achieved, the process of developing an authentic mindset for meaningful aging begins with celebrating your uniqueness as an individual, without which the journey into our senior years could prove to be aimless and futile.

Here's an example of what I mean:

"How come you never share anything in this Super Saturday Event?" I inquired apprehensively of my friend Amit, a fellow resident in the ShantiNiketan retirement community in Tavares, FL.

The Super Saturday Event, held on the last Saturday of every month, has become a ritual in our retirement community. It's an opportunity for residents to share their talents in music, poetry, comedy and other areas in performances of their choice to entertain and educate their fellow residents.

"It is for the talented people, not for me. I just come to listen," Amit responded.

His answer not only surprised me, but also dismayed me as I thought about the plight of many other seniors like him who have spent their entire lives thinking of themselves as being inferior to others, thereby depriving themselves of potential happiness they deserve to enjoy.

"But Amit, you have lived a long and successful life as a professional engineer. Surely, you must have unique talents," I said, prodding further.

"I just did what was required of me. I never thought I had something unique to offer," he replied, apathetically.

Sadly, this type of ignorance about one's personal uniqueness is not limited to seniors; it is prevalent in all phases of human life. The result is a tremendous loss of potential and the squandering of happiness that is so important to have a fulfilling life.

Not recognizing our unique talents leads us to be robotic in our day-to-day functioning, leaving us to *just exist and not live.* So, the first and foremost challenge for all of us is to discover and celebrate our individual uniqueness that contributes to the talents and strengths we have to offer.

Have you ever noticed that some people are outgoing and good at creating a network of friends and supporters while others are shy and interact only when forced to do so? Similarly, some people are good at music and are willing to entertain others, whereas others prefer to listen and enjoy the music. The ability to succeed at something — whether developing friendships or pursuing a talent to be shared — is a strength that is achieved by understanding and nurturing our unique natural gifts, which are our talents.

We humans are amazingly similar, but also uniquely different from one another, physically and mentally. We also view the world and our place in it quite differently than others do, which leads us to chart distinctive courses through our lives.

My wife and I are blessed with 10 wonderful grandchildren. The eldest are twin boys, Arjun and Ravin, who couldn't be more different. Whenever I see or talk with them, I am always amazed at their uniqueness. They were born to the same parents, came into this world only a few seconds apart, and receive the same love from their parents, yet they are quite different. Whereas Arjun is laser-focused on pursuing a professional career and is currently studying molecular biology and statistics, Ravin has explored a variety of fields before deciding to pursue leadership studies at a prestigious business school. Arjun is like a determined person holding a compass to his destiny, while Ravin is like an explorer navigating new paths to get clarity about his destiny. I am confident they will both achieve success in their chosen fields, as long as they continue to realize and revel in their uniqueness.

Just as each of us is physically and psychologically unique, so are the innate abilities each of us have within — our unique natural talents that each of us must identify and nurture based on our individual interests, inclinations and desires.

How do we discover and nurture our talents? Each of us is born with innate talents and abilities that may not be immediately obvious. But as we pursue our interests, inclinations and desires, we discover our talents in different areas and go on to nurture these through the acquisition of knowledge and skills, as well as training and practice. As we develop our talents, they become our strengths and part of what makes us unique.

Your talents are your innate abilities and when nurtured they become your strengths — your uniqueness.

Allow me to share with you my quest to identify my uniqueness.

In 2015, while serving on the board of governors for Leadership Rhode Island, a community leadership development organization, all 15 members of the board completed the CliftonStrengths assessment to help us determine our top strengths. The assessment was provided by Gallup, Inc., an analytics and advisory company that provides strategic consulting to organizations around the globe. The assessment is designed to highlight your top five individual strengths, based on 34 strengths listed in the assessment. Upon completion of my assessment, I learned that my top five strengths in descending order were: *Strategic, Learner, Maximizer, Futuristic* and *Intellection.* A brief description of these strengths is outlined below:

Strategic: *You have ability to sort through the clutter and find the best route. It is a special perspective on the world at large.*

Learner: *You love to learn. Whatever the subject, you will always be drawn to the process of learning.*

Maximizer: *Excellence is your measure. Transforming something strong into something superb is much more thrilling for you.*

Futuristic: *The future fascinates you. You see, in detail, what the future might hold, and this detailed picture keeps pulling you forward, into tomorrow.*

Intellection: *You like mental activity. You like exercising the muscles of your brain, stretching them in multiple directions.*

My first reaction upon learning my strengths was: "So what?" Although the assessment correctly reflected the strengths I exhibited in professional and personal settings, I nevertheless shrugged off the results, figuring there must be countless people on this planet with those same top five strengths. Lo and behold, when I learned more about the assessment, I discovered that only one in 178,000 people has the same top five strengths as mine and only one in 33 million has these top five strengths in the same descending order.

That was amazing to me. With this single piece of knowledge, I suddenly and pleasantly began celebrating my uniqueness as being one of 33 million people on this planet to have these same strengths.

I'm proud of this affirmation of my uniqueness and it is something I point out when, during speaking appearances and in published articles, I encourage others to seek out the qualities that make them unique.

Our ability to get the most out of life is connected to the extent to which we intentionally build strength from our talents.
— Gallup, Inc.

In addition to determining your unique strengths through assessments such as this one by Gallup, you can also identify your top strengths by carefully monitoring your everyday thoughts, behaviors and actions. That's where you will see your top strengths at play. The following are four clues to help determine whether a skill used in an activity is also one of your key strengths:

- *You have an intense craving to do the activity.*
- *You learn rapidly by doing that activity.*
- *You experience intense satisfaction in doing that activity.*
- *You strive for excellence as you continue doing that activity.*

Impediments to discovering unique talents: Why do many people go through their entire lives without knowing their talents and uniqueness? Instead of focusing on what they can do — and do well — they may be focused instead upon their weaknesses, the real or perceived notion that they have no talents to celebrate.

The fact is, a weakness is not necessarily what we can't do, but instead what we don't do well. For example, we may be able to sing, but if we can't sing well, we may view this as a weakness.

Here are some clues to spotting a real or perceived weakness:

- *We feel defensive about our performance:* If we can't perform an activity well, we start blaming somebody or something as a scapegoat. For example, blaming age as an excuse for not able to learn a new language is justification for our weakness of learning.

- *We experience slow learning:* Watching someone play a musical instrument, we decide to learn to play that instrument. However, despite our best efforts, our attempt to learn to play that instrument takes longer than expected and we progress at a snail's pace. We are slow to master the skill.

- *We develop obsessive behaviors:* Despite slow progress in learning a new skill or pursuing an activity, we refuse to give up and keep trying without noticeable progress, rather than abandoning it. We stubbornly pursue new hobbies, even if we don't like them, because we feel compelled to master the skills involved. Imagine that you want to join a bridge club where people are playing the card game to improve mental sharpness while also socializing and having fun. You join the club, however, despite your best efforts, you can't seem to learn how to play the game and you actually find no joy in playing. However, you obsessively keep trying, even when it means sacrificing time that could be spent on other activities you enjoy.

- *We experience loss of confidence:* Not only does it take more time to learn new skills, but we also may lose confidence in our ability to do so. I have met several seniors who decide they want to write a book after hearing me talk about the books I have written. They make a sincere effort, but can't seem to get past the first few pages. Not only do they fail to achieve their dream of writing a book, but they also feel less confident of their ability to try other things — even things they loved to do when they were younger.

As with our strengths, our weaknesses are part of us. We definitely need to know our weaknesses and try to manage them. However, wasting our time trying to turn weaknesses into strengths instead of nurturing our existing talents may be a waste of precious time. According to Donald O. Clifton, the late chairman and CEO of Gallup, Inc., who developed the CliftonStrengths assessment tool used by millions of people around the world, "There is no alchemy for weaknesses. They can be removed, but they cannot be transformed into strengths. The goal, therefore, is to aggressively manage weaknesses, so the strengths can be freed to develop."

A celebration of personal uniqueness: After understanding and believing that you are unique, you must reinforce this belief by openly celebrating your uniqueness.

Every human being, without exception, wants to be recognized and appreciated as an individual. This is an innate need that exists in every phase of our life, and our senior years are no exception. Carol Young, one of those featured earlier in this book as a role model of the dynamic mindset, discovered that volunteer work with nonprofit organizations helped fulfill this need for her. She described it this way:

I shudder to even say this, but I also need to feel respected and appreciated. The twilight years can be depressing, a period when one can easily begin to feel useless. Most nonprofit organizations welcome volunteer time and talents, and the chances are good that the more you feel appreciated, the more you will contribute in return.

Focusing on the following actions can help you celebrate your uniqueness:

- **Strengthen your strengths:** Your talents and strengths are what make you unique, so you must continue to invest time and energy to cultivate them. Dr. Dinesh Shah, another of the role models featured in this book, sets an inspiring example for us on this front. Since discovering his talent for poetry in the sixth grade, Dr. Shah has nurtured this talent throughout his life by writing hundreds of poems in three languages. Even at age 81, he continued to nurture his strength in poetry by reciting some of his poems before an international audience at Harvard University in April 2019.

- **Tout your strengths:** If you don't celebrate your own uniqueness, nobody else will. Blow your own horn, sing your own song or do whatever you're good at — and enjoy doing it. You may think this is pretentious, but others will appreciate your talents — and appreciate your willingness to share them with them. I've seen this in my personal experience, when talking about the books I have written. It was awkward at first, but people appreciated hearing about my experience as an author and learning about the topics I have written about. Public speaking has become a habit for me. Not only does this help reinforce my strengths as a writer and public speaker, but it also has inspired others to do the same.

- **Stop Comparing Yourself to Others:** Celebrate your talents — don't compare them against the talents of others, which can be devastating to your self-esteem. Sure, you should emulate others as you strive to improve, but trying to be like someone else can ruin what makes you unique. The more you compare yourself against others, the more pressure you will feel to be like them or perform like them, which likely will leave you feeling miserable in the end. As President Theodore Roosevelt once said, "Comparison is the thief of joy." Always remember that you have individual qualities and traits that help you stand out in a crowd. By comparing yourself to others and trying to copy them, you become just another person in the crowd.

Many seniors who believe they have no talents, including my friend Amit, who said he had nothing to offer at the Super Saturday Event in our retirement community, are victims of a wrong mindset. Rather than making a conscious effort to find and celebrate their unique talents, they keep comparing themselves to others, cursing their fate and complaining that they have no talent. Instead of comparing themselves to others or complaining, they need to identify, understand and celebrate the strengths they have. Heed these words of wisdom of Oscar Wilde, an Irish playwright, poet and author: **"Be yourself. Everyone else is already taken."**

In conclusion, celebrating rather than ignoring/hiding/resisting/ not acknowledging your uniqueness is a prerequisite for developing your dynamic mindset of meaningful aging. To celebrate yourself, you need to identify and showcase your strengths – those things you do well and enjoy doing. If you're unsure of your specific strengths, use assessments such as the CliftonStrengths assessment offered by Gallup, Inc. Then invest time and expend effort in building and reinforcing your strengths and flaunt them without hesitation – and without comparing yourself to or copying those of others.

It's also important to be aware of your weaknesses and to find ways to manage them, however, your weaknesses will never become your strengths. So, instead concentrate your efforts on building your strengths, which define your uniqueness, which in turn will help provide a clearer view of yourself.

Knowing yourself is the beginning of all wisdom.
– Aristotle

Chapter 16

Discernment

The mocker seeks wisdom and finds none,

but knowledge comes easily to the discerning.

— The Book of Proverbs 14:6

Throughout history, the pursuit of eternal youth and the quest for immortality have often led down a path paved with misinformation and misconceptions that were initially accepted as truths.

For example, research has shown that a Mediterranean Diet, one rich in olive oil, fruits, vegetables, nuts and fish, with minimal consumption of red meats and processed meats, may contribute to a longer, healthier life. This belief is further underscored by the fact that this is the diet of people living in two of the five so-called Blue Zones around the world — Sardinia, Italy; Ikaria, Greece; Okinawa, Japan; Nicoya, Costa Rica; and Linda Loma, CA, in the United States — where the average age expectancy of residents is higher than anywhere else in the world.

While the Mediterranean Diet has proven to be a contributing factor in improving overall wellness, it would be incorrect to assume that this diet is a cure-all that guarantees longevity for all.

Knowing that following the Mediterranean Diet may be conducive to living a long and healthy life is useful, but it should not be considered a panacea that guarantees longevity. That's why it is important to be able to discern the difference between actual facts and various interpretations of them, including those that may lead to inaccurate or blatantly incorrect conclusions.

Discernment is not knowing the difference between right and wrong.

It is knowing the difference between right and almost right.

— Charles Spurgeon,

a renowned Baptist preacher in England

After recognizing and celebrating your uniqueness, your next mandate is to discern the phenomenon of aging, the anatomy and power of your mindset and the key beliefs of a dynamic mindset of aging. The clarity obtained from this discernment will help you thwart myths and misinformation.

Your starting point on this front is to discern the difference between opinions, facts and truths. An opinion is one point of view among many. A fact is a phenomenon which is confirmed by observation, and must be continually proved, tested and confirmed by other observations. Truth is considered ultimate or standard and It does not require any further confirmation. Facts can change, but the truth never changes.

Let us assume a person has been diagnosed with a terminal disease and doesn't have much time left to live. Watch the following explanation of his condition to differentiate between fact and truth:

Fact: This person's condition is serious and his doctor says he has only six months to live.

Truth: Death is inevitable.

Fact: His doctor has identified another medicine that could extend his life expectancy, so he now has two years to live.

Truth: Death is inevitable.

Notice that the facts about this person's longevity have changed, but that doesn't change the truth that death is inevitable.

When someone says or does something, treat that information as being an opinion until it is substantiated as fact. Before acting, check whether that information has been tested and validated. Only then can you treat it as a fact and start believing it. However, be open to testing these facts again and again in order to keep believing them. If at any point, a fact is proved to be wrong, be willing to discard it. On the other hand, if certain facts (beliefs) have withstood the test of time and there is a universal acceptance of those facts, they are realities or truths that need not be questioned.

In the first three chapters of the book, we extensively discussed truths about aging, as well as the formation and functioning of our mindset. We also identified commonly held beliefs and facts that could comprise the dynamic mindset of meaningful aging. It is imperative for each of us to precisely discern, refresh and reinforce them continually. To get started, the following is an encapsulated version of those truths and facts, as well as their validation in the life stories of some of the people profiled in this book.

Four Truths About Aging

- Aging is a lifelong process – not just for the elderly.
- Aging is about living – not ceasing to live.
- We cannot stop aging, but we can choose how to age.
- We continue to create and/or cement our legacies until aging ends.

The predominant myth about aging is that it is a dreaded journey for seniors in the final chapter of their lives, full of suffering with no hope for the future and nothing left to accomplish. In the first chapter of this book, we debunked this myth by showing that aging is not an issue for the elderly – it starts the moment we are born and continues throughout our lives. It is an ongoing process and its purpose is to create/cement our legacies until we complete our journey of life. In a nutshell, aging is all about living, accomplishing and contributing to the welfare of others along the way.

The stories of our role models include shining and uplifting evidence of the truths about aging. For example:

- Dr. Dinesh Shah at age 81 is still pursuing his passions of poetry and science as well as giving back to his community through the three Ts—time, talent and treasure. In 2019, in addition to reciting his poems at Harvard University, he contributed to the development of the next generation of leaders by donating $50,000 to the Hindu American Foundation in Washington, DC, for its summer internship for undergraduate students.
- Carol Young, who retired ten years ago as Deputy Executive Editor of the Providence Journal, is now fully engrossed in providing her time and expertise to many nonprofit initiatives, including Inspiring Minds, a nonprofit education initiative in Providence, RI.
- Dr. Thomas Mathews, an Indian-born medical doctor from West Virginia, established and continues to operate the Belize Spice Farm & Botanical Garden, one of the most popular tourist attractions in this tiny Central American country, even while approaching age 80.

Five Truths About Our Mindset

- We are the product of our mindset.
- Our mindset is enormously powerful.
- We are responsible for our mindset.
- Our mindset can and should by dynamic.
- We can and must constantly refine our mindset.

Our mindset is our mental state – our attitude – that is at the heart of how we perceive our reality and our place in it. It is our disposition that determines our interpretations and reactions to situations, problems and opportunities. These interpretations and reactions translate into our understanding of the way we live our lives. Understanding how our mindset shapes our lives is important at any age, but even more so for seniors who may find themselves feeling powerless in the face of increasing physical and mental limitations.

Our mindset is shaped by our personal beliefs — including our assumptions, experiences and values — and determines how we conduct our lives. Assumptions are those things we take for granted and assume to be true. Experiences are events we have personally observed, participated in or lived through. Beliefs are formed by the values we hold dear, including the intrinsic sense of right or wrong formulated at an early age and developed over the years.

We need humility to accept that our mindset is not static; it can and must evolve. We must be open to constant learning to substantiate or refute our current beliefs. We must be humble enough to acknowledge that sometimes even our most strongly held beliefs can and must change. Without a true awareness of who we really are and an acceptance of the facts of our reality, we may be more inclined to stick with our current beliefs and not be willing to substantiate or refute them.

The truth is that our mindset is shaped by our beliefs and the quality of our beliefs will determine the quality of our mindset, which in turn will determine the quality of our aging.

Five Facts/Beliefs for a Dynamic Mindset of Meaningful Aging

- Aging is an essential quest, not a continual nightmare.
- It is our personal responsibility to make aging meaningful.
- Aging quality is sculpted with effort.
- Continuous learning is the soul of meaningful aging.
- Purposeful passion(s) is vital for meaningful aging.

Guided by the four truths about aging, as well as the five truths about the anatomy and the power of the human mindset, the above five facts (beliefs) of the dynamic mindset of aging are compiled by taking into consideration extensive research of experts such as Erik Erikson, known for his theory, *The Eight Stages of Human Development*; Carol S Dweck, author of the renowned book *Mindset: The New Psychology of Success*; Gene D. Cohen, the founder of the Center on Aging established by the US government and author of the acclaimed book *The Creative Age: Awakening Human Potential in the Second Half of Life*; and Jo Ann Jenkins, the CEO of AARP and author of *Disrupt Aging*; as well as my own eight decades of life experiences, mainly the last 15 years of my life after retirement.

In chapters four through seven, each of the five beliefs of the dynamic mindset of aging is discussed in detail by sharing the life experiences of seniors who have learned to develop and live with those beliefs. These chapters also discuss the traits that can help you cultivate and reinforce those specific beliefs.

The story of Dr. Paul James, covered in chapter four, is an example of aging being an adventurous and purposeful quest. In the story of retired Air Marshal S. Raghavendran, covered in chapter five, we explore the sculpting of a better quality of life at all ages. In this chapter, we also reviewed the fundamental elements required to sculpt a better life – attitude, adaptability and audacity. In chapter six, in the story of Dolores Cummins, we find the secret to navigating new and uplifting paths. In chapter seven, in the story of Vishwakant Mankodi, we see how a successful businessman and entrepreneur struggled for years to achieve his dream of singing with a harmonium, but committed himself to learning this skill in his later years to realize that dream. In chapter eight, through the amazing life story of Mai Donohue, a poor girl growing up in war-torn Vietnam in the 1960s who went on to become a teaching assistant in the United States, we see the power of aligning our passions with a larger purpose of helping others to achieve fulfillment in our lives.

Through the stories of five other people, you can see the power of the assimilated five beliefs of a dynamic mindset of aging. The following excerpts from their stories demonstrate the manifestations of that power:

Enrique Brouwer – A Cuban Gift: *I am in my early 70s, while Baldev is a few years older than I. Not once in our correspondence or conversations have we ever talked about anything other than the future, including exciting ideas for the years to come. This outlook is a consequence of having a dynamic mindset that propels you into the future and keeps your mind and body committed to the business of living life in the moment; life as an active manifestation of what is good and worthy within us; and life as a journey of discovery. The dynamic mindset is not a frenetic, headlong race towards a false and naïve denial of inevitable death. It is not a vapid 'whoever dies with the most toys wins' view of life. It is a celebration of life through assertive personal actions, continuous improvement and unrelenting personal responsibility. This results in periods of reflection, a celebration and an affirmation of life at its best. The gains attained by following the dynamic mindset in our advanced years are consequential and significant.*

Vijaya Srinivasan — A Warrior Missionary: *Aligning passion with purpose is important when it comes to giving your life deeper meaning. For me, feeling purposeful is all about being of service to others and making their lives better. During my career, I have grown to understand the value of being a lifelong learner, which is also the secret to aging dynamically. I have also learned that my beliefs affect how I see myself and others, and I have made a commitment to having a positive mindset in terms of always looking for the good in others. Personal responsibility is really critical when* *aging because you alone are totally responsible for your life. I have learned that life is not easy; it is like a river on which you travel with lots of winding turns along the way. We are here to travel on that river, learn along the way and enjoy what we can. Life's challenges grow our spirits and bring us closer to the divine and our suffering can even be a gift in helping us to focus on what truly is important. Life is a challenge, a pilgrimage, a journey, a mission. My personal mantra is: Life is about giving love and helping others and wanting to make a difference in any way I can and having strong faith in God.*

Dr. Dinesh Shah – A Relentless Voager: *It became more and more clear to me that my ceaseless efforts to pursue my passions of science and poetry and helping others are not ascribed to any secret or formula, but they are attributed to the power of my attitude (mindset) with which I have played and continue to play the game of my life.*

Dr. Thomas Mathew – A Habitual Novice: *As long as my mindset remains dynamic and keeps me motivated to take responsibility for my situation, learn every day and shape a better quality of life for myself, my wife and all the people on the farm, I will not have the time to worry about any additional wrinkle, any additional year added to my age or any additional challenge to my existence, and the journey of my life will continue unabated to create joy and meaning.*

Carol Young – A Do-gooder: *With the benefit of hindsight, my post-retirement journey, now in its ninth year, reflects the realization that I am happiest when I'm productive and harnessing my passions. You might say that I have unknowingly embraced elements both of the dynamic mindset and the eternal truths about aging, concepts introduced earlier in this book by my friend, Baldev Seekri.*

In Conclusion: Being able to discern between opinions, facts and truths, and having the precise knowledge (discernment) of the phenomenon of aging, anatomy and the power of human mindset, as well as having the validated beliefs to build your dynamic mindset of aging are essential to shield you from the many myths and misinformation about aging that are so rampant in our society. It is important to fully embrace a dynamic mindset that will enable you to adapt to the inevitable challenges of your senior years.

When we are mature in discernment, we overcome deception.
— John Bevere, best-selling Christian author and founder of Messenger International

Chapter 17

Reflection

Learning without reflection is a waste.
Reflection without learning is dangerous.
— Confucius

Within a week of giving a talk on creativity in the later years of human life, I was approached by at least five seniors who asked me what creative things they could do to make life better for themselves and their fellow residents in our retirement community in Florida. Although I was elated to see their enthusiasm for finding creative ways to improve our community, I also was saddened by their inability to look within themselves for ideas and instead seek help from external sources.

The inability to seek answers from within is not limited to seniors; it is prevalent among many adults in our society. Without this ability for self-reflection, it is very difficult to recognize your personal triggers for gratification and genuine happiness, thus making it difficult — if not impossible — to develop and reinforce your dynamic mindset. It is imperative that you understand what self-reflection is, learn how to do this and make it a part of your regular routine.

Throughout history, prominent philosophers have practiced and preached the virtue of self-reflection and contemplation. According to Confucius, "By three methods we may learn wisdom: First by reflection, which is the noblest; second, by imitation, which is easiest; and third by experience, which is the bitterest." According to Samuel Taylor Coleridge, the great English philosopher and poet, "There is one art of which man should be a master — the art of reflection."

Self-reflection involves deep thinking — analyzing our experiences, actions, feelings and responses to events in our lives. It is the art of thoughtful pondering about every aspect of our lives. The learning we gain from self-reflection gives us the opportunity to either validate and strengthen our existing beliefs and continue following our chosen path with increased energy and enthusiasm, or it signals the need to change our beliefs and transition to a new way of thinking, feeling and acting to create a better path for our journey. In either case, self-reflection helps us keep our mindset dynamic in every phase of life, including our senior years.

The power of self-reflection in determining whether to continue, modify or chart a new path after retirement is evident in the lives of those featured in this book. Let us review two examples:

Vishwakant Mankodi: *Reflecting on my past achievements, including learning new and difficult things, made me aware that the primary reason for the successes in my life was my unflinching dedication and disciplined effort to learn — and that was missing from my quest to learn to sing while playing the harmonium. I realized that I had half-heartedly tried to learn before, but had given up too soon. So, I realized it was time to focus on achieving my goal — this time with the zeal for learning that had helped me achieve success in the past.*

Without serious reflection, Mr. Mankodi could never have realized his goal of learning how to sing while playing the harmonium when he was in his 80s.

Enrique Brouwer: *By reflecting on my life at the onset of my retirement, I realized that I did not need to reinvent myself in my golden years because I realized that what has truly always made me happy is to be of service to others; that I have donated my life to others.*

216

It was the power of self-reflection that led him to his chosen path for his life journey, one in which he is committed to serving others. As a result, he is experiencing genuine happiness in his seventies.

Making self-reflection your habit: Even for those who understand the benefits of self-reflection, many have a difficult time making it a habit. Self-reflection is a matter of focusing on every aspect of your life to gain a clear perception and understanding of who you are by examining your thoughts, feelings and actions. By conducting this self-analysis on a regular basis, you can better assess who you are, what you're doing and what you want to do differently moving forward.

Here are some simple tips to make self-reflection a habit that can help you determine whether to continue or modify the path you're on, or whether to chart an entirely new path in your remaining years:

- Set aside some time when you can be free of distractions and obligations. Have a pen and notepad — or your computer or tablet — handy to record notes.

- Focus on a recent experience, letting it run like a movie in your head. Note your emotions about the experience, good and bad.

- Think about what you could have done differently to increase the positive emotions and reduce the negative emotions you felt.

- Consider how this experience impacted your life: Is it something positive you want to pursue? Is it worth investing additional time, so you can modify your actions/response? Or is it time to reassess how and why you were involved in this experience and chart a new course for the future?

This is not rocket science; it's very simple to do. So why do many people fail to self-reflect? They may not understand that for something to become a habit, it must be part of your natural disposition or it must be learned and practiced until it becomes part of your routine.

Sustained commitment is the key and this will happen only if you meet the previously described requirements for commitment: desire, determination and discipline. You need desire to develop the habit; determination to succeed in developing the habit; and discipline to regularly practice self-reflection. A half-hearted commitment will not get you to your goal of making self-reflection a habit. You need to be fully committed to making this happen.

Once reflecting on your emotions and actions becomes easier and starts to become a habit, you also can start to reflect more deeply about other aspects of your life. Through self-reflection, you can develop clarity about your passions and your purpose in life, which often go undetected by most people. Knowing and pursuing your passions and your purpose are vital to keeping your mindset dynamic.

Unveiling your passions and purpose through self-reflection: There are many interpretations of passion and purpose. Many people use these terms interchangeably and, at times, erroneously.

To be clear, your passion is something you love to do that also provides satisfaction. Satisfaction is felt when your desires are met. You can find satisfaction while enjoying the things you love to do, such as playing golf, drinking fine wines, driving a Ferrari, writing a book or increasing your net worth. These are examples of individual passions that can provide satisfaction, based on an individual's interests. Passion brings excitement to our day-to-day functioning. As Oprah Winfrey says, "Passion is energy — feel the power that comes from focusing on what excites you."

Purpose, on the other hand, is using your passion to benefit others, which in turn can provide genuine happiness. Using your passion to make a positive difference in the lives of others not only gives you a sense of purpose, but also provides satisfaction and genuine happiness, for you and others.

Aristotle once said, "Happiness is the meaning and the purpose of life, the whole aim and end of human existence." Happiness isn't just a fleeting feeling — it's a state of mind that results from your actions and behaviors. Voluntarily giving your time, talent or treasure to improve the life of an individual or an entire community is incredibly empowering and provides genuine happiness. This can be achieved in a variety of ways; showing compassion to others, fostering a child and providing care to fellow seniors are some of the purposeful actions that can provide a sense of happiness.

To have a meaningful and happy life, you need both passion and purpose. Purpose is the reason for your journey. Passion is the fire that lights the way.

Discovering your passions and your purpose entails reflecting on your life and determining which activities give you satisfaction as well as those that provide genuine happiness. This discovery isn't based on a single reflection, but rather continuous self-reflection until you notice a pattern. Please allow me to share with you how I discovered sources of my passions and purpose.

If you recall from the introduction of this book, a couple of years after my retirement at age 65, I was searching for a new identity to establish my relevance in the retirement world. After facing a few setbacks by trying unfamiliar endeavors, I started to seriously reflect on my life in an attempt to find a new direction for the journey of my retirement life. For about six weeks, I regularly and rigorously reflected on every phase of my past professional and personal life and wrote down the actions that generated satisfaction or happiness for me. When I tabulated the results of six weeks of reflection, I discovered an amazing pattern regarding the sources of my satisfaction and happiness:

My Satisfaction and Happiness

Actions	Satisfied	Happy
Learning new facts and ideas.	X	
Sharing my knowledge with others.	X	
Giving my resources and time to others.		X
Transforming good situations to great.	X	
Expressing Gratitude to others.		X
Risk-taking with courageous actions.	X	

Baldev K Seekri

If you look closely at this chart, you can easily see what makes me feel satisfied and/or happy. All of the actions and choices (learning, communicating, transforming the situation and risk-taking) that give me personal satisfaction are focused solely on me. These are my **passions**, which I pursue to prove my personal significance. They are my natural dispositions – my unique gifts. Constantly nurturing them gives me immense satisfaction.

However, as the chart shows my acts of giving to others and/or expressing gratitude are the sources of my genuine happiness. These happiness-generating actions are centered on others, not on me. I don't do these things for my personal satisfaction, but rather for the benefit of others. They represent my **purpose**, which is to make a positive difference in the lives of others.

Understanding the authentic sources of my passions and purpose, I felt rejuvenated when it came to charting a new direction for my retirement life. That's why I decided to be an author, so I could pursue my passions of learning, communicating and transforming. Writing became the focus of my new-found pursuit in retirement. When I published my first book, *Organizational Turnarounds with a Human Touch,* in 2011, I not only learned a lot as a result of my research, but I was also able to communicate that learning, along with my own experiences, to my readers. I also streamlined many turnaround processes and terminologies to make them simple and thought-provoking for others interested in this process. While I felt great satisfaction by pursuing my passion, I didn't forget my purpose – to enlighten others. I also expressed my sincere gratitude in the book to those people who helped shape me as a leader. The happiness I experienced by being able to express my gratitude to my mentors in the book was priceless.

In your passion resides your satisfaction and your purpose generates your genuine happiness.

Constant reflection of your actions and choices is a nifty way to discover the triggers of your satisfaction and happiness. Knowing your passions and your purpose is not only exciting, but also is vital in terms of building and reinforcing your dynamic mindset.

Although continual self-reflection is a necessity in every phase of human life, it's paramount in our senior years for two very important reasons:

- This is the time of our life when we aren't sure of the direction we want to go in our protracted uncertain life.

- Given that we will likely encounter increased and unanticipated physical and cognitive adversities during our older years, we need a mindset of aging that is dynamic, sturdy and wise to guide and encourage us to adapt to our rapidly changing realities.

By extracting wisdom from our lifelong experiences, self-reflection not only makes our minds stronger and more agile, but also helps us to correct the misgivings and misconceptions we tend to develop in our later years. Think for a moment: without serious reflection, what type of journeys could Vishwakant Mankodi, Dr. Dinesh Shah, Enrique Brouwer and I have had in our retirement lives?

Having realized the absolute necessity of constant reflection in your advanced years, you must expend time and effort to learn to make self-reflection your habit and practice it with total commitment. Your advanced years give you a lot of time to do this, especially in retirement. Starting to practice self-reflection may seem strange and even difficult, but please take my word for it: you will find it quite interesting and beneficial in developing your plan for your later years.

As you get comfortable doing self-reflection and it becomes a habit for you, start reflecting more deeply to discover your true passions and purpose. Please remember: *Passion is what you love to do and gives you satisfaction in doing it while purpose is what you do for others, resulting in genuine happiness in the process.*

In Conclusion, identifying your passions and purpose through self-reflection will help you identify your triggers for satisfaction and happiness more clearly. This makes your mindset more dynamic and sturdier as you continue your life's journey with confidence and positive anticipation. Without serious personal reflection, you may find yourself following someone else's life journey while wondering where you are going.

Without deep reflection, one knows from daily life that one exists for other people
– Albert Einstein

Chapter 18

Alignment

As you grow older, you will discover that you have two hands:
one for helping yourself, the other for helping others.
— Audrey Hepburn

"What will you do now?" I asked Dr. Patel, anxiously.

"I am figuring it out and you will know it soon."

That was the cheery response of Dr. Dinesh Patel, an 83-year-old resident of our retirement community, who recently experienced a dramatic decrease of eyesight due to chronic glaucoma. Although Dr. Patel was not officially practicing medicine in our retirement community, he was still highly respected for sharing his medical knowledge with residents who needed information to deal with their various ailments. He also gave regular talks about the prevention of old-age infirmities and he was a trusted ally of the ailing, willing to visit and communicate with their doctors and hospital staff. Dr. Patel was also an ardent bridge player who would always find time in his busy daily schedule to play a game of cards. He was a champion bridge player who competed in surrounding towns and won a few tournaments playing the game.

Being quite close to him, it was natural on my part to worry about the deterioration of his vision and the resulting impact this would have on his quality of life, given how active he was. It was difficult for me to see him struggling with basic tasks, such as reading and driving his car.

Dr Dinesh Patel (standing) explains the intricacies of playing bridge to seniors

To my great relief, my worries didn't last long because I discovered that Dr. Patel was pursuing a passion that didn't require perfect eyesight – he was keeping quite busy teaching the game of bridge to other residents of our community. In fact, his classes were so successful that bridge playing had become a favorite pastime for an increasing number of residents there. So, while he had curtailed reading, driving and other favorite activities, he was busier than ever with his bridge classes and was quite jovial as a result.

This story is an excellent example of the importance of having a dynamic mindset, which helps you adapt to changes in your personal circumstances. Dr. Patel's handling of adversity – his failing eyesight – by pursuing a new passion – teaching his fellow residents how to play bridge – can serve as inspiration for people of all ages, especially seniors in their later years and others just approaching retirement.

The biggest danger to our dynamic mindset of aging is our inclination to capitulate to the adversities that may restrict our physical, mental and emotional abilities as we age. The increasing frailty of our bodies and slowing of our brains can easily cause us to revert to a classic mindset of aging. Rather than believing that aging represents an opportunity for adventure – a quest that enables us to seek happiness by creating our legacy – adversity may make the path ahead appear as a dreaded nightmare, leaving us feeling helpless and dependent upon others until life ends. For many of us, it's easier to give up rather than to find an alternative path to a good quality of life in our later years. That's why Dr. Patel is such an inspiration. In my experience, few people respond to adversity the way Dr. Patel has, with a dynamic mindset of aging that allows them to continue living with positive anticipation of what's to come.

What made Dr. Patel an exception? Sure, he had been a respected geriatric physician in Maryland for 35 years; had participated in health panel sponsored by the National Institutes of Health; and had taught numerous medical students over the years. While many other seniors may have similarly impressive credentials, few could match Dr. Patel's ability to keep his dynamic mindset of aging intact in the face of increasing physical limitations caused by his advanced age.

The secret that Dr. Patel and few others have discovered is articulated in these words of Oprah Winfrey: "I've come to believe that each of us has a personal calling that's as unique as a fingerprint – and that the best way to succeed is to discover what you love and then find a way to offer it to others in service, working hard and also allowing the energy of the universe to lead you."

Ms. Winfrey's comments apply to all of us, at any stage of our lives. What she is suggesting is that if you combine your passion – something you love to do — with a larger purpose — giving service to others — you will find success in all you do.

This is exactly what Dr. Patel has done. Prior to experiencing the recent setback caused by his loss of eyesight, he was pursuing his passion of playing bridge, which he loved. At the same time, he was devoting time serving his fellow residents by providing medical advice, promoting healthy habits and lifestyles and accompanying them to their medical appointments. Now, faced with physical limitations that restricted his ability to read, drive and even walk, he has found a new way to give purpose to his passion by teaching others the game of bridge. This is a classic example of using the dynamic mindset of aging to achieve success and find happiness in your later years.

> The real joy in life comes from finding out your true purpose
> and aligning it with what you do every single day.
> — Tony Robbins,
> author, philanthropist and life coach

As Enrique Brouwer, one of those profiled in this book, reminds us: "This journey of aging is not a linear or tidy proposition. There are negative aspects associated with growing old, such as physical limitations caused by the process of aging." We must constantly realign our passions to an appropriate purpose, especially as we face limitations in the ones we have been pursuing. Unlike our passions, which generally come naturally to us and we love pursuing them for our own personal satisfaction, our purpose can take on many forms as long as it is a selfless act of helping others, which also provides us with genuine happiness as a result.

Mai Donohue, who was depressed and despondent after suffering a ministroke in 2015, is among those who seriously reflected on the impact of changes in her life and decided to change course. "Either I could be angry and unhappy for the rest of my life or grateful to be alive," she said.

MEANINGFUL AGING

Self-reflection and creativity are two indispensable and complementary ingredients for aligning passion with a purpose. Aligning our different passions with a larger purpose is extremely important for seniors to navigate the quickly changing realities caused by the natural deterioration of our physical and cognitive capabilities. In the preceding chapter, you have learned how to self-reflect and make this a part of your routine. Hopefully, you have become quite proficient in that and are now ready to learn about creativity.

Creativity in Senior Years: One of the myths responsible for seniors discarding their dynamic mindset is a belief that our brains deteriorate faster than our bodies in our later years, making us less creative. This causes some seniors to believe they have nothing but dull days ahead. This myth has persisted for generations. Consider this quote from 1842 by Sydney Smith, a British clergyman: "Old age is a wasteland of sleepless nights and unexciting days." But 100 years later, Ellen Glasgow, a Pulitzer Prize-winning novelist, helped debunk this myth by declaring: "In the past few years, I have made a thrilling discovery – that until one is 60, one can never learn the secret of living. After 60, one can live with one's entire being. The entire being is our creative spirit which empowers us to participate in life as a journey of exploration, discovery and self-expression." She was 67 years old at the time.

That pronouncement by Ellen Glasgow, combined with the increasing life expectancy of seniors, helped stimulate interest in the creative ability of seniors. Nearly 60 years she made that statement, Dr. Gene D. Cohen, a pioneer in the field of geriatric psychiatry and founding director of the Center on Aging, Health & Humanities at George Washington University, published a book called *The Creative Age: Awakening Human Potential in the Second Half of Life,* in which he encouraged older people and their families to continue to engage in creative activities, saying research had shown that these types of activities helped people live longer and healthier lives.

Dr. Cohen's book is a treasure trove of valuable information regarding the psychological and physiological aspects of creativity in our senior years. According to his research, Dr. Cohen concludes that human creativity is highest in the second half of human life as we gain maturity, experience and wisdom. Essentially, he describes the four phases of human potential from midlife through our later years as follows:

Human Potential Phases in Later Years

Phase	Feelings/ Behavior
Evaluation Phase (40s to age 60)	*We begin to re-evaluate our sense of purpose; our path in life. We consider questions such as: Who am I? Where I am going?*
Liberation Phase (Mid-50s to Mid-70s)	*We have liberating feelings and thoughts:* If not now, when? Why **not?** What can they do to me? *We start taking risks.*
Summing-up Phase (70s or older)	*There is an urgent desire to find a larger meaning in our lives by looking back, summing up and giving back through our creativity.*
Encore Phase (80s and older)	*We want to reaffirm our place in the world by creating/cementing our legacy(s).*

According to Dr. Cohen, each of the above four phases, which are defined by our chronological age and circumstances, promotes new possibilities later in life. As we cross the threshold of middle age, **The Reevaluation Phase** during our 40s, 50s and 60s, we begin to evaluate our lives, including what we've done or accomplished in the past and our plans for the future. Some call this a midlife crisis. But it's also an invitation to pursue our creativity in later years.

As we march on with our lives, we enter the second phase, **The Liberation Phase,** from our mid-50s to mid-70s. This is when we develop a sense of personal freedom, feeling free to speak our minds and share our experiences. This feeling of liberation nourishes our creative juices, providing us with the incentive to try something different with our lives.

The next phase, **The Summing-up Phase,** occurs mostly at age 70 or older. In this phase, we develop a strong desire to add a larger meaning to our life. We reflect upon our life and sum up our passions and become eager to give meaning to them. Our focus starts to shift from doing this to pursue personal satisfaction to finding happiness through our contributions to others. We reflect on our lives to determine what our true passions are and we become eager to use those to help others. According to Dr. Cohen, this is the peak time of our creativity, which also makes it the perfect time to find ways to align our creative passions with the larger purpose of helping others. This often entails giving of our time, talent and treasures to support worthwhile causes, such as sharing our creative expressions and wisdom by writing a book or essays or by participating in community activism. The creative outburst in this phase of our lives helps us focus on navigating the last chapter of our life.

The last phase of human potential, **The Encore Phase,** which includes those in their 80s and older, is focused on realizing our impermanence and reaffirming our life through ingeniously creating and cementing our legacies. Our brains and our imaginations benefit from the process of creating/cementing our legacies. As a reminder, a legacy is defined as follows by Robb Lucy, author of *How Will You Be Remembered?*: "A legacy is something I create that connects and enhances lives now and will continue to positively affect others when I am gone."

My three takeaways after extensively studying Dr. Cohen's research into the creativity of seniors can be summarized as follows:

- Humans are creative by nature and their creativity peaks in the second half of their lives due to maturity, experience and wisdom.
- Curiosity about our life and courage to make changes are essential ingredients to incite and nurture our creativity.
- The more creative we are, the easier it will be to align our passions with a larger purpose of helping others, which in turn can lead to genuine contentment.

Sadly, in my retired life, I have observed that many seniors not only shun being creative when facing adversity, but also are completely unaware of the fact that they are in the optimum period of life in terms of using creativity to try new things or optimize existing creative pursuits. This ignorance and the hesitation to pursue new options can unfortunately force them to make the transition from a dynamic to a classic mindset of aging; instead of embracing aging to help others, they start viewing it as a dreaded nightmare.

In conclusion, to keep our our mindset dynamic as we age, and to continue the journey of aging in pursuit of genuine happiness, we have to adapt to the changing realities in our later years by reflecting on our lives to identify our true passions and creatively align these passions with a larger purpose of benefiting others. This alignment with the power of reflection and creativity can be a game-changer for seniors, allowing them to transform their lives and seek new horizons. Such was the case for American folk artist Anna Mary Robertson Moses, better known as Grandma Moses. When arthritis made it impossible for her to continue her favorite pastime of embroidery, she took up painting at age 78. She exhibited her work at famous galleries around the world until well into her 90s, and she continued painting until a few months before her death at age 101. This is also what Dr. Patel did at age 83, when he began to teach others the game of bridge when deteriorating eyesight impacted his ability to pursue routine activities such as reading and driving. This is also what YOU can do. As a senior, at any stage of your aging journey, you also can embrace the fact that your creativity has not diminished in your senior years. On the contrary, it has blossomed to its peak level. By believing this fact, you can follow in the footsteps of people like Grandma Moses and Dr. Patel and become inspired to use your creativity to provide a new direction in your life and align your passions with the larger purpose of serving and helping others. You will thank your dynamic mindset when adversity strikes and you face it courageously and enjoy a happier, healthier life as a result.

The more your passion, vision and purpose are in alignment, the easier it is to move with inspired action.
— Michelle "Tamika" Washington, a transgender woman and community advocate

Chapter 19

Resilience

When you come to the end of your rope,

tie a knot and hang on.

— Thomas Jefferson

Ever wonder how some people recuperate faster and bounce back stronger from their physical and emotional challenges as compared to the majority of us who succumb to adversity and become more feeble in body and spirit?

Think about the story of Vijaya Srinivasan -- A warrior Missionary, earlier in the book, who confronted death twice and roared back stronger after a double-lung transplant and is now living a meaningful life helping others, such as her work with the ladies' group in our retirement community and similar undertakings. Where did she get her unbridled enthusiasm and energy to face those overwhelming ordeals? The answer lies in **resilience** – the human ability to bounce back from adversity or any significant source of stress. It helps us to bend and not break. In fact, resilience is much more than bouncing back; it is the ability to bounce back even stronger from whatever life throws at you. It also is the skill that helps us prevent adversity in the first place and endure it should adversity occur.

Conventional wisdom is that resilience gets cemented in our personality in our childhood and we live our entire lives with that fixed level of resilience. But research shows that resilience is a process that can be learned. The American Psychological Association defines resilience as "the process of adapting well in the face of adversity, trauma, tragedy, threats or significant sources of stress. Resilience is not a trait that people either have or do not have. It involves behaviors, thoughts and actions that can be learned and developed in anyone." This distinction is important because, while personality traits tend to be fixed, processes are inherently fluid, which means seniors can learn and develop resilience.

Why is resilience so important in our senior years? Although facing adversity occurs at every phase of human life, the frequency of adverse situations tends to increase greatly as we journey into our advanced years. Increasing frailty caused by the degeneration of our physical wellbeing increases our susceptibility to a host of physical ailments. For example, for most of my adult life, I relied primarily on one doctor — my primary care physician. Since retirement, I've had to consult with a number of specialists to deal with different ailments. These additional medical issues and doctor appointments have created additional stress, which I need to deal with as I march on with my life. Similarly, we face an increasing amount of mental and emotional adversity as we age, especially as we lose close friends, face chronic illnesses and experience declining cognitive abilities with every passing year. As a result, our place in society seems to become ambiguous and burdensome.

Stress caused by these increased physical and psychological challenges can lead to depression, helplessness and isolation. Resilience is our protection from the wrath of these overwhelming physical and emotional challenges in our advanced years. Accordingly, resilience, though needed in every phase of our life, becomes an indispensable necessity if we are to have any chance for a meaningful and productive life in our remaining years. It becomes imperative for seniors to understand the key domains of resilience and learn to develop every aspect of them.

Domains of Resilience: In my research, the most simple and appropriate discussion about resilience is provided by Dr. Amit Sood, a former professor of medicine and former director of the Mind-Body Medicine Initiative at the Mayo Clinic. In his book, *The Mayo Clinic Handbook for Happiness: A Four-Step Plan for Resilient Living*, Dr. Sood explains that resilience has four domains—physical, cognitive, emotional and spiritual. Let me present a simple explanation of those domains and how they are vital for seniors.

Physical Resilience: To maintain the best possible health to remain strong and healthy and be able to recover quickly from illness or injury. Taking personal responsibility for our own health by maintaining healthy habits such as an active lifestyle, healthy eating, adequate sleep, nurturing relationships and timely medical and preventive care is paramount in our advanced years. Consider the experience of Enrique Brouwer, featured in the chapter A Cuban Gift—Noblesse Oblige, who says, "This journey of aging is not a linear or tidy proposition. There are negative aspects associated with growing old, such as physical limitations caused by the process of aging. I was a track and field standout in high school and college, and I have always enjoyed being physically active. While I can no longer run a record-setting sprint in the quarter-mile, I still walk approximately three miles each day and far more than that on most days. I also do resistance training at the gym three days a week. Both activities are not only good for my body, but for my mind, too. Staying active is also consistent with my personal mission statement in that the walking I do is to serve myself and my dog by keeping us healthy, and going to the gym with my wife and exercising together helps keep us in harmony as a couple."

Cognitive Resilience: To maintain focus amid stress. Imagine that you have an important appointment with your doctor at 8 a.m. and you have to take a particular medicine before leaving for the appointment. At 7:30 a.m., you need to leave to get to the doctor's office on time, but first you need to take your medicine. You look in the medicine cabinet, where you normally keep your medicine, but you can't find it. You become agitated and shout to your wife, asking where your medicine is. She looks in the medicine cabinet where she quickly finds it. It was right there in front of you. Sound familiar? This happened to me just recently and I am sure you've experienced a similar instance of losing focus in stressful situations.

This loss of focus in our advanced years is a common saga in the lives of many seniors and our struggle on this front gets more intense if we don't do anything about it. Keeping mentally sharp by learning new things and perfecting your hobbies can help make you become more resilient on a cognitive level.

Emotional Resilience: To approach life's challenges with a realistic, flexible and balanced disposition while having good control of your emotions. Emotional resilience involves experiencing positive emotions most of the times (joy, calm, satisfaction with the past and hope and optimism for the future) and quickly recovering from negative emotions (anger, sorrow, shame and fear). In my experience, seniors are quite focused on becoming more resilient physically and mentally and spend considerable effort on these fronts while doing little to improve their emotional resilience. Poor emotional resilience can dilute the improvements in physical and cognitive resilience since negative emotions don't allow sustained improvement in those efforts. Cultivation of emotional intelligence needs to become a top priority for seniors if they aspire to experience happiness in its true form in the journey during the last phase of their lives.

After years of research, Dr. Sood found that whenever there is a stressful episode brewing negative emotions, we must attempt to embrace one or more of the following five feelings:

Gratitude: *Stay positive - not negative:* Be grateful for the experiences in your life. Try to focus on what went right and not what went wrong. When things go wrong, try to be grateful that what happened wasn't as bad as it could have been. With practice, your gratitude threshold changes and you can learn to become grateful for the little things.

Compassion: Recognize that we all struggle with battles, large and small. We deserve each other's kindness.

Acceptance: Realize that all of us, ourselves and others, are human. We have imperfections and are fallible. Be more accepting of the real or perceived failings of yourselves and others.

Meaning: As we age, we often ask ourselves three questions: Who am I? Why I am here? What is this world? Remember these answers: I am here to serve and love every role I play in life. I exist to make this world a kinder, happier place, and I am here to take advantage of all the opportunities to learn and contribute in this world.

Forgiveness: This is your gift to others and ultimately to yourself. Forgiveness frees your mind, allowing you to discover greater meaning and happiness.

Spiritual Resilience: The ability to find an anchor in higher meaning and selfless perspective despite facing adversity and disappointment in your life. Mahatma Gandhi remained anchored in the higher meaning by preaching nonviolence, while risking his life many times. Nelson Mandela practiced forgiveness and compassion rather than being consumed by revenge and violence. Taking refuge in the almighty when adversity isn't warded off with sincere effort are examples of spiritual resilience.

Barriers to Increasing Resilience: Over time, I have observed that as we age together, my wife recovers from illness and other adversities much faster than I do. Her level of resilience far exceeds that of mine. Is this due to her genetic makeup or something else? After spending decades studying how people deal with setbacks and illnesses, Dr. Martin Selig-man, a psychologist who is Director of the Positive Psychology Center at the University of Pennsylvania and is commonly referred to as the founder of positive psychology, describes in his book *Authentic Happiness* the three Ps that can inhibit recovery:

Personalization – the belief that we are at fault.

Pervasiveness – the belief that an event will affect all areas of our life.

Permanence – the belief that the aftershocks of the event will last forever. "Everything is awful. It is my fault that it is awful. My whole life will be awful."

As we face adversity, we all are shackled by these three Ps to vary-ing degrees.

In my case, whenever I face any infirmity, even catching a common cold, it seems like the end of the world for me. I blame myself for doing something wrong to catch that cold (personalization), brood about the possibility that the infection will spread to other parts of my body requir-ing X-rays of my chest or a biopsy of my lungs (pervasiveness); and due to my age, I keep assuming this will never go away (permanence). My wife, on the other hand, goes through the suffering of her infirmities by taking medicine and embarking in preventive measures without blaming herself nor indulging in what-ifs. By the time she is recovered, I am still dragging on miserably and fearfully through my ordeal.

Sure, our different genes and health conditions play a role in our sus-ceptibility to catching illnesses. However, it is the relative grip of the three Ps that dictates how long and how much we will suffer before we recover. In other words, the biggest impediment or barrier to our resilience in the face of adversity is the grip of our beliefs towards these three Ps: per-sonalization, pervasiveness and permanence.

Dynamic Mindset and Resilience in Aging: How will developing a dynamic mindset help us to increase our resilience during aging? As discussed, poor resilience is the result of our adherence to the three Ps, which can make us overly pessimistic. According to Dr. Seligman, pessimists have a particularly pernicious way of dealing with their setbacks and frustrations. In other words, their negative outlook or mindset about aging attracts and solidifies the three Ps. He explains that Pessimists are up to eight times more likely to become depressed when bad events happen. They also tend to have worse physical health and live shorter lives. In contrast, optimists, those with positive attitudes, tend to have a strength that allows them to interpret their setbacks as surmountable, particular to a single problem and resulting from temporary or short-term circumstances.

An increasing amount of research shows that having a positive attitude about aging increases resilience in later years. According to a recent study led by Dr. Jennifer Bellingtier, formerly of North Carolina State University, which examined the attitudes of seniors aged 65 to 96, having a positive attitude about aging was associated with greater resilience. The study asked participants about any stress or other negative emotion they felt in their day-to-day lives, as well as existential questions such as whether they thought they were as happy or useful in their later years as they were when they were younger. The results were clear:

"We found that people in the study who had more positive attitudes toward aging were more resilient in response to stress," Bellingtier says.

The dynamic mindset of aging is built upon positive beliefs about old age that minimize our temptation to embrace the three Ps and increase our resilience to the challenges we face in our advanced years. These positive beliefs include viewing aging as a journey to find happiness and not a dreaded nightmare; accepting personal responsibility for continual learning to sculpt a better quality of life and denying the sense of entitlement to be cared for by others; and realizing the gift of additional years of life to be able to create/cement our legacy to make this world a better place. The more we develop a mindset with these positive beliefs, the more resilient we will become to manage and face adversities of our senior years.

Collective Resilience: As more seniors choose to live in retirement communities, their collective resilience may be as important as their individual resilience. According to the 2010 US Census, only 3.1 percent of seniors were nursing home residents at that time. Rather than moving to a nursing home, more seniors are opting to remain in their own homes with in-home care and support, or they are seeking independent and assisted living in retirement communities. These communities commonly include apartments, condominiums and single-family homes. Residents include seniors who may not require assistance with daily activities or 24/7 skilled nursing care, but they may benefit from the convenience of having services such as grocery stores, banks and doctors' offices built into these communities, as well as senior-friendly surroundings and the increased availability of social opportunities that many of these independent senior living communities offer. Independent senior living communities are especially popular among seniors who wish to downsize or travel freely without the burden of maintaining a home, as well as those who seek seasonal relocation from the harsh cold winters or sweltering heat of summer.

Collective resilience in communities such as these is powered by the sharing of experiences, narratives, hopes and power. This is especially true in the five Blue Zones — specific regions around the world where people are known to live longer and happier lives. These include Sardinia, Italy; Ikaria, Greece; Okinawa, Japan; Nicoya, Costa Rica; and Linda Loma, California. These areas are known for having close-knit communities of seniors and their collective resilience to withstand adversities is said to be one of the key reasons for the longer, happier survival of the residents who live there.

A Resilient Community: For the past five years, my wife and I have spent four to six months each year in the ShantiNiketan 2 independent retirement community in sunny Florida, where we are considered snow-birds escaping the harsh winters of the northeast United States, where we live the rest of the year. With great admiration, I have observed that the collective resilience of this community continues to build with each passing year, generating a fulfilling retirement experience for its residents. Most of the people who live here are retired first-generation Indian profes-sionals who had successful careers in medicine, management, engineering, business and other fields. Together, they have created an environment that enriches the lives of everyone who lives there, including taking steps to improve every aspect of their personal and collective resilience. This includes engaging in *moderate exercise* to increase physical resilience; sharing personal experiences and expertise with fellow residents and playing intellectually stimulating games together to build cognitive resili-ence; celebrating rituals and festivals from different parts of India to fos-ter appreciation for and acceptance of each other to improve emotional resilience; and participating in devotional music and group singing to nur-ture spiritual resilience. These are just some of the regular activities in the community.

Most residents voluntarily participate in these activities, which helps build the collective resilience of the entire community. For example, as an author, I give two or three presentations each year to more than 200 res-idents about my research pertaining to meaningful and joyful aging.

*Here's a photo of one of my presentations at the **Shantiniketan 2** retirement community, where I'm discussing creativity in the later years.*

A recent example of the increased resilience of this community occurred in February 2019, in the heart of winter, when the population peaks with the arrival of all the snowbirds. About 75 percent of the community residents are members of a food club that has served three fresh meals of authentic Indian vegetarian food each day at a very reasonable cost for residents. Other residents prepare their own meals at home. This arrangement had been in place since the community was founded in 2012, however the food club abruptly shut down at the end of February 2019, when the person overseeing the food club abruptly quit, removing his management team, equipment and food supplies, leaving two chefs without the means to prepare any food. Given the specialized nature of Indian food, there was no nearby alternative to secure the services and supplies needed to feed those who had come to rely on the food club for their meals.

Rather than panicking, most residents of our community stepped up to fill the void — including people who weren't even members of the food club. Many of the women took over the responsibilities of cooking while many of the men brought fresh vegetables from a nearby farmer's market and bought serving supplies from a local department store. Many members donated money and provided interest-free loans to finance the effort. It was nice to see the community joining hands to address this issue

Women from ShantiNiketan 2 preparing fresh vegetables before a meal.

These volunteer efforts were so successful that there was no interruption in the availability of fresh food. Within a matter of weeks, we streamlined the process by establishing a full-time team of volunteers with clear responsibilities for operations, financing, quality, logistics and safety. The quality of the food improved and the cost for residents also decreased slightly. Marveling at the success of the volunteer efforts, residents decided to carry on the experiment by changing the volunteer team every three months. For the next 12 months, the food operation ran seamlessly with all-volunteer teams until the board of directors for our community assumed full responsibility for food operations and appointed a full-time manager.

What caused this remarkable experience in the ShantiNiketan 2 community? The collective resilience of the community, fostered by their efforts to constantly strengthen their practices and rituals to enhance the physical, cognitive, emotional and spiritual resilience of the community.

In conclusion, resilience is an indispensable necessity in our advanced years. We need resilience to face, prevent, endure and bounce back stronger from a multitude of adversities, especially those instigated by the deterioration of our physical and mental capabilities. It is next to impossible for seniors to build resilience without a positive attitude about aging. The five beliefs of the dynamic mindset — aging as an adventurous quest for genuine happiness, personal responsibility, continual learning, shaping better life quality with effort and making it purposeful by creating/cementing a personal legacy, are necessities for continuing to develop and grow a positive attitude as we age.

Seniors can do themselves a great favor by understanding what resilience is, including its four key aspects — physical, cognitive, emotional and spiritual, as described in this chapter. That knowledge, combined with adopting a mindset of dynamic aging at all times and in all situations, will help you feel more energetic and enthusiastic, allowing you to face rather than fear every adversity in your advancing years.

> **Our greatest glory is never falling,**
> **but rising every time we fall.**
> **— Confucius**

Epilogue

Meaningful Aging comes down to this: Every phase of human life provides challenges to manage and opportunities to harness, and our advanced years are no exception to this reality. For many seniors, unfortunately, the last phase of their lives, from retirement to their finale, is mostly a matter of existing rather than living with purpose and hoping to experience contentment.

The bare truth is that we cannot control the ultimate end, as nobody lives forever; however, it is within our power to choose between merely existing or living with hope in our advanced years. That choice is dictated by our mindset toward aging and, more specifically, our attitudes about growing older. Aspiring to live with hope in finding contentment requires a dynamic mindset built upon the belief that the last phase of our life is a quest for contentment, not a nightmare. We must assume a personal responsibility to exert effort to shape the quality of our life, rather than assume that we are entitled to be taken care by others. Most important, having a dynamic mindset reinforces our duty to constantly learn and pursue purposeful passions while creating and reinforcing our legacy.

Drawing from the wisdom of 10 seniors from varied walks of life who have understood and developed a dynamic mindset about aging and are living their lives with positive anticipation, coupled with the insight of experts and my personal experience during 15 years of retirement, I identified and presented the five essential mandates for developing, refreshing and reinforcing your own dynamic mindset of aging. These mandates, outlined in section three of this book, are the key to making your journey after retirement meaningful and joyful. Knowing these mandates isn't enough. You need to thoroughly discern them and develop the sustained motivation needed to put them into practice at all times and in all situations. Remember what Confucius said: *I hear and I forget. I see and I remember. I do and I understand.*

The basic distinction between sustained and fleeting motivation is the disciplined commitment to practice. You must structure your effort in such a manner that it becomes your habit and manifests itself voluntarily. Any structured effort will produce desired results only if we break the overall task into achievable segments. So, taking a lesson from the Mayo Clinic's stress-free living program, in which they structure five components of increasing emotional resilience during the first five days of the week, we are going to structure the practicing of our five mandates — celebration, discernment, reflection, alignment and resilience — during the first five days of our week, every week, from Monday through Friday.

Monday: Celebration

This is the day to remind yourself — and celebrate the fact — that you are a unique individual, worthy and capable of seeking happiness in your golden years. You need to acknowledge that your uniqueness is hidden in your talents (your natural abilities) which are manifested through your strengths (activities you perform very well and enjoy doing). Monday is your day to acknowledge and bolster your strengths; to shun the temptation of comparing yourself with others; and to share your strengths with others while also learning about their strengths. These are the pathways to enhance your consciousness of your uniqueness so you can celebrate this gift and experience the genuine happiness you truly deserve.

Tuesday: Discernment

This is the day for you to do two things:

First, remind yourself that aging is a lifelong process and not earmarked as calamity for the elderly; it is not a matter of solely existing, but rather living in the pursuit of happiness by creating and/or reinforcing our legacy(s). The quality of our aging can be improved through positive attitude, adapting to the changing realities of our advanced years and setting audacious but realistic goals.

Second, please pay attention to your thoughts, behaviors and actions during the day and ascertain if they conform with the five beliefs of a dynamic mindset. In case you find yourself deviating from any of the beliefs of the dynamic mindset in real life, please refresh your understanding by reading the mandate on discernment.

Tuesday is your day to ascertain and correct your understanding of the truths about aging and to reinforce the five beliefs of a dynamic mindset that are essential for aging meaningfully.

Wednesday: Self-reflection

Wednesday is your day for self-reflection. You must first remind yourself that although reflecting on our experiences, actions and choices are beneficial in every phase of our human life, it is paramount in our senior years to adapt to the fast-changing realities of our physical, mental and emotional capabilities.

Next, you must make sure that you clearly know the sources of your satisfaction (passions) and your happiness (purpose) and that you are pursuing them diligently in your daily functioning. Remember that passions are the activities you love to do – those things that give you personal satisfaction and purpose is what you do selflessly for others in order to experience genuine happiness.

Reflect on the actions of your previous week and make a list of the activities that gratified you and the ones that gave you a great feeling of genuine happiness. Is there any new passion or purpose which you were not aware of? If so, please note it on your list. As you continue recording your activities on subsequent Wednesdays in the next six weeks, check to see if you notice a pattern emerging and pursue your new passion or purpose accordingly. Wednesday is your day to reaffirm the importance of self-reflection and use it to reaffirm the triggers of your passions and purposes.

Thursdays: Alignment

This is the day to remember that your ability to pursue your passions increases significantly when your passions are also aligned with a larger purpose of making a positive difference in the life of others. Also, it is the day to remind yourself that as your limitations increase with your advancing years, you must keep a dynamic mindset to find creative ways to enable you to align your appropriate passion with a larger purpose, which can help thwart the limitations you may be facing. Remember what Anna Mary Robertson, also known as Grandma Moses, did in her late 70s, when she realized her physical limitations were inhibiting her ability to pursue her love of embroidery. With her dynamic mindset, she took up painting, instead, becoming a world-renowned artist whose paintings were displayed in the finest art galleries in the United States and Europe before and after her death at age 101. This is also what Dr. Dinesh Patel, a retired geriatric physician did, when at age 83 he began teaching the game of bridge to residents of his retirement community after his deteriorating eyesight severely impacted his ability to pursue his normal activities of reading and driving.

This is what you – a senior at any stage of your aging journey – can do by embracing the fact that your creative power in senior years has not withered way; on the contrary, it has blossomed to its peak level. On Wednesdays, you must conduct a sanity check to make sure you are not capitulating to your limitations in your aging journey, but instead are creatively aligning your appropriate passions with a larger purpose of helping others, while also becoming more energetic and enthusiastic.

Friday: Resilience

Friday is the day to remind yourself that your resilience is an indispensable necessity in your advanced years, enabling you to face, prevent, endure and bounce back stronger from a multitude of physical and psychological adversities. It is next to impossible for seniors to build resilience without a positive attitude about aging. The five beliefs of the dynamic mindset are the cornerstone for developing and growing a positive attitude.

You can do yourself a great favor by understanding the four aspects of resilience – physical, cognitive, emotional and spiritual – and building upon them by taking care of your health; indulging in activities that sharpen your mental focus; controlling your emotions; and looking to the higher power when your own efforts to manage personal adversity falter or fail. Please understand that, by far, increasing emotional resilience is paramount and you should work on improving it by practicing gratitude, compassion, higher meaning, acceptance and forgiveness.

The five mandates outlined in this book are your pathway to comprehend, develop and reinforce your dynamic mindset of meaningful aging. The degree you rely on them in your day-to-day thoughts and actions will dictate the quality of your aging life and the happiness you are seeking.

During the four years I have spent writing this book, I have interacted with hundreds, if not thousands, of seniors and have listened to them describe their feelings and challenges in their aging journeys and the ways there were coping with them. I was also privileged to hear their remarkable approaches for making their journeys meaningful for themselves. All of those valuable counsels helped not only to make my own aging journey more manageable and enjoyable, but also led to the design of the dynamic mindset of aging and the five mandates that can be used as a roadmap for all seniors to use to develop and reinforce their dynamic mindset.

As an author, public speaker and ardent advocate of interactive learning, I have made a number of presentations to groups of seniors on the relevant topics about aging such as the aging process, creativity, resilience, self-reflection and many others during the course of writing this book. Encouraging members of my audience to share their points of view and asking questions about their concerns has always nurtured my own learning. Without divulging any names, I want to share five intriguing questions that might relate to your personal situations as a senior:

Question: I am not keeping so well. I (at age 82) have accepted aging as a disease with no real cure. *it looks like my time is almost over. Why should I learn about developing a dynamic mindset of aging now?*

Answer: Understanding our situation is commendable, but a capitulation to our difficult situation without expending effort to make it better is lamentable. No doubt, with our advancing years, we all, without exception, are going to face increasing adversities instigated by the continual degradation of our physical and psychological capabilities, as well as frequent emotional traumas due to the loss of our close relations and colleagues. There can't be any denial of this inevitable truth. We — all seniors — are in the same boat, and gradually, the boat is going to get more and more wobbly.

We can't control the end, but we can definitely choose to make the balance of our journey relatively manageable and purposeful. A dynamic mindset makes us look beyond our limitations and take personal responsibility for managing and improving our situation. In this book, reading the story of Dr. Felix Silverstone, a national leader in geriatrics who at age 87 could feel his own mind and body wearing down, will not only give you the courage to manage your limitations, but will also inspire you to find purpose in your remaining life. What sustained Dr. Felix Silverstone, a national leader in geriatrics for five decades, after suffering physical and cognitive decline, was having a purpose: to be of service, in some way, to those around him. He formed a journal-reading club for retired physicians, guided a young geriatrician through her first research study and facilitated a survey of attitudes about aging.

Additionally, most seniors don't understand that their most valuable ally, which can give them the courage and purpose in their trying years, is their God-given resilience: physical, cognitive, emotional and spiritual. Understanding and nurturing resilience, especially, emotional resilience, can make all the difference when it comes to moving towards the end with a positive anticipation rather than just existing fearfully. Using the five tools to increase emotional resilience – gratitude, compassion, acceptance, higher meaning and forgiveness definitely provides a sense of calmness and courage that enables us to make the most of our remaining time. Always remember these words of Thomas Jefferson: *When you come to the end of your rope, tie a knot and hang on.*

Question: *I am 64 and still working, enjoying my professional status and success. I have no time to think about what my retirement*

*life will be, but I assume it will take care of itself. Why worry now —
and why should I read this book about* **Meaningful Aging?**

Answer: It's perhaps more important for you to read this book
than those who are already undertaking the journey of the last
phase of their lives. Your mindset is a microcosm of a multitude of
other near-retirement seniors who think your way, only to find
themselves surprised when their retirement life becomes aimless
and meaningless after a few years. I am a living proof of this reality, since I started my retirement life with the mindset you have
and I paid a heavy price, financially and psychologically, before
I found my passion and purpose in achieving a fulfilling retirement. So, too, was the case with Ms. Carol Young, the retired
deputy executive editor of the Providence Journal, whose story
appears in this book. She also struggled to find relevance in her
retirement and later found it through her volunteer work with several nonprofit organizations. It is highly recommended that, in the
hustle and bustle of your professional and personal life, you find
some time to understand the need for, anatomy of and power un-
leashed by a dynamic mindset about aging. Later on, you will be
glad you did.

Question: *I am 70 years old and retired three years ago. Being retired means a life of freedom for me — doing what I want to do,
when I want to do it and the way I want to do it. Why should I give
that up to pursue meaning and purpose in retirement?*

Answer: Your question reminds me of a famous quote by Frie-
drich Nietzche, a German philosopher: *People don't want to hear
the truth because they don't want their illusions destroyed.* It seems
that you may be living in an illusory world, thinking your carefree

life will continue unabated. Although I support your pursuit of happiness — if freedom is your definition of happiness — sooner or later, when your freedom is threatened due to physical and psychological limitations, you likely will start to realize that retirement life is not just about chasing pseudo contentment; it's about living with purposeful passions and experiencing true fulfillment, which brings authentic happiness. There is still time for you to learn the truths about aging and the need for a dynamic mindset in your advancing years before your illusory world starts to crumble and you find yourself helpless and lacking direction. Please heed these words of *Miguel De Cervantes*, the famous Spanish author of *Don Quixote, which* has been translated into more than 140 languages: *Forewarned, forearmed; to be prepared is half the victory.*

Question: *Recently, a relative of mine committed suicide at age 79, as he couldn't bear the pain of his protracted physical decline and what he described as unbearable boredom. How can this book help avoid this type of tragic ending for seniors?*

Answer: I am sorry to hear about your relative's situation, which is very unfortunate. Some seniors can't cope with their personal situation and make the unfortunate decision to end their lives. Studies show the suicide rate among seniors increases dramatically with age. According to the data from the federal Centers for Disease Control and Prevention (CDC), the suicide rate for people age 65 to 74 was 15.6 per 100,000 seniors. That number jumped to 18 for seniors age 75 to 84 and to 20.1 for seniors over age 85.

Developing a dynamic mindset based upon truths about aging, as outlined in this book, will definitely help seniors avoid embracing the mindset of a victim in the face of increasing challenges, both physical and psychological. Heed the words of Steve Maraboli, a bestselling author who writes about what happens when we find ourselves in the grip of a victim mindset: *The victim mindset dilutes the human potential. By not accepting personal responsibility for our circumstances, we greatly reduce our power to change them.*

This is exactly what happens to many seniors contemplating suicide — they give up their power to change their circumstances. The dynamic mindset of aging changes the attitude many seniors have about aging: *It is a quest for contentment and fulfillment, not a nightmare. We must assume personal responsibility for shaping the quality of life through constant learning, adapting to our changing circumstances and pursuing purposeful passions to create or enhance our legacy.*

It is not only our responsibility, but also our solemn duty to make our senior relatives and friends aware of the importance of having a dynamic mindset of aging so that their attitude towards the last phase of life changes from fear of a frightening death to a kinder and more dignified end-of-life experience.

Question: *For me, life before retirement was all about looking forward to a bright and carefree future, and to achieve goals not yet attained, not a frightening journey toward a dreaded dead end. How can we get excited about this last phase of our human existence?*

Answer: If you had posed this question to Dr. Leila Denmark, the oldest practicing physician in the United States when she retired in 2005 at the age of 103, or to Eamon de Valera, who served as the president of Ireland at age 90, or to Mohr Keet, the South African who set the Guinness World Record for being the oldest person to bungee jump at age 96, or to countless other seniors who attained their greatest achievements in the last phase of their human lives, they likely would have scoffed at your inquiry.

But sadly, you are not alone in your concerns. Many, if not most, people have this type of mindset towards the last phase of our lives. The reality is that each of us has the same goal in every phase of human life — to accomplish something worthwhile, while achieving personal growth and contributing to the well being of others and society at large. This last phase of life is no exception to this reality. Although our physical and emotional capabilities decline with advancing age, our ability to find creative solutions to thwart our limitations is at its height due to our accumulated experiences and wisdom.

So, take it from me: The mission remains the same, but the strategies required to carry out the mission change during the different phases of our lives. Rest assured, the last phase of the journey of life can be as exciting as every other phase, provided we have the courage and foresight to understand the truths about aging, as well as being able to adopt the beliefs of a dynamic mindset of aging, as outlined in this book.

In conclusion, the goal of writing this book was to convince you that embracing the proper mindset is vitally important to the aging process. We all have the choice as to whether to merely exist or to live with meaning and purpose, which ultimately will give us satisfaction and fulfillment in our final years. By conducting extensive research into the intricacies of the aging process, by identifying and exploring the lives of 10 great seniors from different walks of life who shared their mindsets of living with purpose and genuine happiness, and by sharing my personal life experiences of eight decades — especially the last 15 years after my retirement, I have been able to provide you, the readers, a path to comprehend, develop and reinforce a dynamic mindset of aging. This mindset will help you navigate the journey of your golden years with positive anticipation and, hopefully inspire you to pursue your purposeful passions and experience the contentment and fulfillment you truly deserve.

I feel quite confident that by developing and reinforcing your dynamic mindset by following the five mandates— celebration, discernment, reflection, alignment and resilience — at all times and in all situations, all seniors will see their golden years as not a dreaded nightmare but as an adventurous quest for fulfillment which we all deserve.

Good luck – and may the power of your dynamic mindset be with you.

Index

About the Author

Baldev K. Seekri is the Author of *Organizational Turnarounds with a Human Touch* and *Seizing Success-How Mindset Makes it Happen.* He is also the writer of three manifestos on *Perceptions, Inspiration,* and *Success* at Changethis (1-800-CEO-Read).

In his forty years professional experience prior to retirement, Mr. Seekri is accredited with transforming numerous organizations around the globe from struggling to the high performing eminence. He retired at age 65 after thirty years of distinguished service with Texas Instruments Inc. as General Manager. After retirement, he served on the board of governors of Leadership Rhode Island (LRI), a nationally recognized community leadership development organization for six years (from 2011 to 2017).

At age 80, he continues to be an active author, business leader, and a sought-after speaker. He lives with his wife Kamlesh in Attleboro, Massachusetts in the summer and in Tavares, Florida in winter in the ShantiNiketan Independent retirement community. More on baldevseekri.com